TRICK OR TREATMENT:

HOW AND WHEN
PSYCHOTHERAPY FAILS

In words, as fashions, the same rule will hold,
Alike fantastic if too new or old:
Be not the first by whom the new are tried,
Nor yet the last to lay the old aside.

Alexander Pope,
Essay on Criticism, Part II

Trick or Treatment:

How and When Psychotherapy Fails

by
Richard B. Stuart, Ph.D.
Professor, School of Social Work
University of Michigan

Foreword by
Joseph Wolpe, M.D.
Professor of Psychiatry
Temple University Medical Center

Research Press
P.O. BOX 3327
COUNTRY FAIR STATION
CHAMPAIGN, ILLINOIS 61820

TRICK OR TREATMENT:

HOW AND WHEN
PSYCHOTHERAPY FAILS

Copyright © 1970 by Research Press Company
Second printing, 1971
Third printing, 1973
Fourth printing 1973
Fifth printing 1974

Copies of this book may be ordered from the publisher at the address given on the title page.

ISBN—0—87822—052—6

Contents

Foreword

A book like this one, laying bare how current psychotherapeutic practices often harm the patients they are supposed to help, is long overdue; yet it could not have been written until recently. What has made a successful critique possible is the accumulation of evidence that neurosis is a phenomenon of learning and that schizophrenic behavior is largely learned even if there is a biological substructure for it.

Psychoanalytic theory, which has dominated psychiatric thinking for half a century, attributes the symptoms of "functional" psychiatric illness to hidden internal sources. The existence of these hidden processes has never been demonstrated. Nevertheless, the psychoanalytically oriented therapist assumes their presence in every case and then purports to derive a detailed image of them from the patient's verbalizations. This is not difficult to do, and, rewarded by the approval of colleagues, soon becomes a confident habit. Dr. Stuart shows how conclusions drawn from these ratiocinations not only fail to bear therapeutic fruit, but often actually hurt the patient. Besides the direct harm that wrong treatment can do, indirect damage can be done by pejorative inferences that may be conveyed quite blatantly or by innuendos borne on such phrases as "may be significant."

Dr. Stuart's main concern has been with some particularly widespread and rather subtle avenues of iatrogenic distress. But the theories and practices he criticizes also lead to harm in other, grosser ways. Physicians, when unable to establish a diagnosis of physical illness, often refer patients to psychiatrists for assessment and possible treatment. If a psychological attribution of the illness results, as it frequently does, one of its effects is to block further medical investigation of a condition that may have an organic basis after all. I think of a woman with persistent backache who turned out to have a spinal meningioma, of another whose attacks of dizziness were really due to Meniere's disease, and of a case of frigidity that I found to be due to a painful vaginal lesion, after the patient had wasted two years in psychoanalysis. There is a far cry between determining that symptoms *could* have a psychological origin and establishing that they do. Failure to trace symptoms to physical disease is not a sufficient basis for psychotherapeutic action. It is necessary also to have positive indications of psychiatric illness—an impossibility when this depends on relating a presumed hidden process to the symptoms that are manifest.

The knowledge that neurotic reactions are lawfully tied to specifiable antecedent conditions completely changes the diagnostic situation (as well as the therapeutic prospect). It gives us the power positively to decide when psychotherapy is indicated. We conclude that a symptom has a psychological basis only when we have evidence that it is controlled by stimuli, either directly or indirectly. Attacks of asthma, for example, can only be regarded as having a psychological basis when they are related to emotional disturbances which, in turn, are consistent consequences of particular stimulus conditions.

It is fortunate that this important exposition of iatrogenic influences was undertaken by someone with a mind as incisive as and a pen as expressive as Dr. Stuart's. I hope that everyone who does psychotherapy will read this book, for it has the power to persuade many to exchange "Rx for failure" for "Rx for change."

Joseph Wolpe, M.D.
Philadelphia, Pennsylvania
September, 1969

Introduction

Much of the material contained in this book was originally
presented at the Conference on Behavioral Technology
which was sponsored by the Department of Psychology,
University of Oregon, Eugene, Oregon, on July 10-12, 1968.
The author wishes to express his gratitude to those who
organized and participated in the conference as they, however
unknowingly, stimulated the development of this material.

The author also wishes to acknowledge the invaluable
editorial and secretarial assistance of Miss Lynn Nilles, the
critical help graciously offered by Drs. Edward Heck and
Al Siebert, the scholarly assistance of Mr. Peter Loeb and
Mrs. Elizabeth Hawley, and the indulgence of his wife,
Freida, and sons, Jesse and Toby.

The reader whose biases run contrary to those of the
author will notice that most of the studies and reviews mentioned are of a negative character, while many studies with
positive results have been omitted. This is the consequence of
a deliberate selection process based upon one practical consideration and two philosophical arguments. On the practical
side, it must be recognized that the literature potentially
relevant far exceeds the limitations of one small book. On the
philosophical side, the first argument was provided by Blalock
(1964), who suggested that "causal thinking belongs completely on the theoretical level and that causal laws can never
be demonstrated empirically [p. 6]." This means that one
cannot hope to "prove" a generalization, particularly those

related to inner states which depend upon long inferential chains. This leads to the second argument, which is found in the work of Dukes (1965). He pointed out that while proof of a generalization may be beyond the scope of the empirical methods, disproof or qualification can be based upon only a single contrary instance. When these negative materials are produced by authors in professional publications, one must be mindful of the hesitance of both individuals and the media to publish reports which reach negative conclusions. The appearance of many such reports must be construed as a serious challenge to the veracity of the generalizations associated with dispositional diagnosis.

It should be pointed out that validation or rejection of psychiatric hospitalization or of psychotherapy is a very complex task owing to the complexity of the treatments. Psychiatric hospitalization is influenced by the characteristics of the patient and his family, by the availability of therapeutic personnel and their characteristics, by the unique organizational features of each hospital, and by the nature of treatment and evaluational criteria employed. In a recent excellent account of psychotherapy research, Strupp and Bergin (1969) have indicated the interacting roles of setting, therapist, patient, treatment and research criteria in evaluating psychotherapy. At best, then, the research summarized here (pro and con) can be taken to be only an approximation of the effects of intervention.

With large scale validational research a matter for the future, it is imperative that hospital and individual therapists maintain close evaluational control over their daily activities with patients. This can be done through an objectification of treatment goals and measurement of the effects of treatments designed to achieve these goals. The general responsiveness of therapists to systematic treatment and to data is therefore a matter of central importance if patient well-being is to be protected. This book will review some of the efforts to achieve these safeguards and some of the responses by leading proponents of differing therapies to the challenge of meeting this obligation.

Throughout this book, several assumptions will be made. First, it will be assumed that in most instances, social behavior will be continued if it leads to positive social consequences and discontinued if it leads to negative social consequences. Second, it will be assumed that "positive" and "negative" are terms which have functional meaning—that is, a consequence is positive if it accelerates the response which it follows, and it is negative if it decelerates the response which it follows. For example, the silent interest of a therapist in his patient's tale of woe may be a positive consequence which leads the patient to tell more of his problem, in one instance. The same patient might tell his tale to another person (or to the same person at a different time) and might stop talking when he meets with silent interest.

This leads to the third assumption—that positive and negative consequences may vary from person to person from day to day. This means that effective treatment must be consistently responsive to shifts in the behavioral characteristics of each patient, with very general assumptions about human behavior being restricted to use as the general guidelines of treatment.

For a fuller description of the behavioral assumptions underlying this book, the reader is referred to either of the following excellent texts:

C. B. Ferster and M. C. Perrott, *Behavior Principles* (New York: Appleton-Century-Crofts, 1968).

J. R. Millenson, *Principles of Behavioral Analysis* (New York: Macmillan, 1967).

References

Blalock, H. M. *Causal inferences in nonexperimental research.* Chapel Hill: University of North Carolina Press, 1964.

Dukes, W. F. N=1. *Psychological Bulletin,* 1965, 64, 74-79.

Strupp, H. H. & Bergin, A. E. Some empirical and conceptual bases for coordinated research in psychotherapy: A critical review of issues, trends, and evidence. *International Journal of Psychiatry,* 1969, 7 (2) 18-90.

1

The Medical Model and Iatrogenic Illness

Sam has always been chosen last on a baseball team because he swings under the ball and strikes out a great deal.

Bob reads at a low level of proficiency and eats a very narrow range of foods.

Bill and Margaret married after a brief courtship and have had frequent quarrels since they were married.

Should Sam, Bob, and/or Bill and Margaret be offered psychotherapy or behavior therapy with an educational focus for their problems? More information would naturally be needed to answer this question, but one key element in the decision will be found in the nature of the inferences which are drawn by the professional observers whose help they seek. For example, Sam might be viewed as suffering from "an intense lack of self-esteem associated with faulty ego development," while Bob might be seen to suffer from "a severe character-ological problem, with features of anger, passive-aggressive qualities," or Bill and Margaret might be viewed as "both pre-oedipal and hence pre-sexual in orientation so that each retreats from adult sexual-social responsibilities." In each instance, it is likely that psychotherapy would be prescribed.

On the other hand, Sam might be viewed as suffering from problems in hand-eye coordination and posture control; Bob might be seen as suffering from problems in visual tracking and from eating behaviors which are under faulty environmental control; and Bill and Margaret might be viewed as lacking knowledge about how to successfully influence each other. A professional who took this view might recommend a behaviorally specific educational program for each of the individuals, rather than psychotherapy.

If psychotherapy were offered, it would be based upon the assumption that the observed problems are surface manifestations of underlying personality problems. Treatment would, in most instances, be oriented toward eliminating the pathogenic personality conditions or at least toward strengthening the defenses of the healthy portion of the personality against the destructive forces of the unhealthy elements. Whatever the long-range result of this treatment, it is likely that Sam would suffer continued alienation from his friends, Bob would fall further behind in school, and the relationship between Bill and Margaret would worsen. If psychotherapy were successful, these temporary losses might be acceptable. If it were not successful, on the other hand, then these losses must be regarded as serious problems.

If behavior therapy were offered, it would be based upon the assumption that the observed problems are the result of either a history of inadequate learning or the present operation of a defective environment which does not stimulate and/or reinforce acceptable behavior. Treatment would be oriented toward provision of the needed training or toward bringing about the necessary environmental changes. Temporary changes in behavior are likely to occur, but *if* the problems were indeed manifestations of underlying personality problems it is possible that the same or other problems of greater or less severity would emerge soon after.

At the basis of the theories of psychotherapists and their arguments against the behavior modification approach lies the so-called "medical model" (Ullmann & Krasner, 1965). This model assumes that an apparent problem of human behavior is a symptom of an underlying pathogenic condition in much the same way that elevations of fever or white corpuscle count are manifestations of infection in the body. To continue the argument, it is assumed that unless the pathogen is removed, a greater number of possibly more severe symptomatic problems will result.

This model has obviously worked well in the treatment of physical ailments, and this success is perhaps the chief reason for the willingness of psychotherapists to accept the approach. A second reason may be the simplicity of the model with its appeal of parsimony. A third reason might be the emotional appeal of the argument (Scheflen, 1958), which carries with it an implicit guarantee that once the pathogen has been named it can be removed, resulting in cure.

In order for the model to be legitimately applied to psychotherapy, it must be shown to be appropriate and useful. There is good reason to believe that it is neither. First, its appropriateness has been challenged. Turner and Cumming (1967) have argued:

> The explicit attitude or mental habit of viewing behavioral deviations as symptoms of some inner pathogenic element, which must be identified through accurate diagnosis in order to know how to treat it, reflects an assumption that organic disease and psychological disorder are structurally and etiologically isomorphic. Such an assumption is neither theoretically nor experimentally defensible [p. 43].

In addition to questioning the validity of applying medical theory to psychotherapeutic problems, one might also question the logic of such an attempt. The great philosopher of science, Alfred North Whitehead (1925), referred to this tendency to attribute all phenomena to extensions of the natural order as a vestige of medieval thought and, as such, vulnerable to a range of unscientific weaknesses. McConnell (1968) has carried this argument further and has noted a parallel between the concept of *animus* in medical biology and the use of the medical model in psychotherapy. He indicated that just as it was necessary to purge physicians of the notion that the body was the temple of the soul in order to free the science for such advances as heart transplants, antibiotics and cancer cures, so too will it be necessary to eliminate unscientific spiritual notions from psychotherapy if the problems of so-called "mental illness" are to be overcome.

Beyond arguments about the legitimacy of the metaphor drawn between the medical model and psychotherapy, one can also argue that there is voluminous data to support the view that the medical model is not useful and must be purged from our scientific approaches to behavior change. The subsequent chapters of this book will review extensive support for this argument, based upon literature which demonstrates the inability of the model to generate a system for classifying disorders which reaches a respectable level of reliability and validity; the failure of the model to yield an intervention approach which is effective; and even the failure of the model to provide a valid method of refuting erroneous hypotheses about problematic behavior.

Criticisms of Behavior Therapy Based upon the Medical Model

Apart from the weaknesses inherent in the medical model, its proponents have used it as a basis for criticisms of alternative methods of treatment—most notably behavior therapy. Reports of the success of behavior modification have ranged from relatively unsystematic accounts of the numbers of patients who have benefited from the uncontrolled efforts of a single therapist (Wolpe, 1958) to studies that utilize the most sophisticated designs currently available for outcome research (Paul, 1966). These reports have generally encountered either of two responses from disbelievers. One group attacks the methodologies upon which the studies are based, disregarding the more scientific studies entirely (Breger & McGaugh, 1965; Bruck, 1968), while, paradoxically, these same authors recommend acceptance of the theory implied in conventional psychotherapies despite the fact that it is supported by even less verification (Carter & Stuart). But these criticisms are not central to the major thrust of behavior therapy, and may be taken as reasonable suggestions that more rigorous research methods should be employed.

A second group of critics attacks the idea central to behavior therapy: to remove the "symptom" is to remove the illness (Kanfer & Saslow, in press; Ullmann & Krasner, 1965). These critics postulate that man is analogous to the internal combustion engine and that when any of the manifold outlets (symptoms) are eliminated without a reduction of energy (dynamic illness), further system breakdown can be expected (Bookbinder, 1962; Greenson, 1959; Spiegel, 1967). Many cogent responses to this argument have been offered by behaviorists: Some have indicated the failure of this expectation to be demonstrated (e.g., Baker, 1967; Yates, 1958), some have challenged the validity of the analogue (e.g., Wiest, 1967), while still others have offered behavioral explanations for the observation—and expectation—that behavior therapy may sometimes be unsuccessful (Cahoon, 1968). As an example, Stuart (1968) has sought to explain the failure of certain attempts at behavior modification in their having tried to decelerate problematic responses before first attempting to accelerate adaptive responses. When this is done and a therapist removes an important source of reinforcement from a patient's life, the patient will naturally seek to replace this satisfaction. Unless the therapist has taken the precaution of encouraging the occurrence of acceptable responses, the patient may indeed replace one unacceptable response with another. Failures such as this provide a source of data which enables behavior therapy to undergo the self-corrective process essential in a science.

Beyond defending behavior therapy, however, it is important to point out that failure and/or deterioration may be experienced by patients who undergo psychotherapy. Allen Bergin (1966), in a very important recent paper, reviewed the literature pertaining to the outcome of psychotherapy and concluded:

> . . .although there tends to be no difference in the average
> amount of change between experimentals and controls, there
> does tend to be a significant difference in *variability* of
> change. . . . Typically, control subjects (Ss) improve somewhat,
> with the varying amounts of change clustering about the mean.
> On the other hand, experimental Ss are typically dispersed all
> the way from marked improvement to marked deterioration
> [p. 235].

If this conclusion is correct, it can be said that psychotherapy
may prove beneficial to some and harmful to others. To state
the negative case more strongly, psychotherapy which is
offered to counteract illness may in fact often contribute to
the exacerbation of illness in many patients. Illnesses of this
sort, which are caused by the treatment, have been termed
iatrogenic illnesses and must be of focal concern to the so-
called "healing professions."

Iatrogenic Illness as a Consequence of Medical Treatment

One of the most ancient and most precious precepts of the
medical profession is *"Primum no nocere"*—"First of all do
no harm" (Chapman, 1964). It is therefore not surprising that
the medical profession has given careful consideration to the
problems of iatrogenic illness and medical malpractice.

Iatrogenic illness may result from the predicted or unantici-
pated consequences of treatments which are properly chosen
and correctly executed. Some of the effects may result despite
the fact that the quality of treatment offered is the best
available. In these instances, diagnostic problems may be so
complex as to exceed the competence of the best diagnostic
processes, treatments may be experimental in character, or
illnesses may be so grave as to warrant daring treatments. In

10

other cases, iatrogenic illness may result from malpractice or the failure to use average skill and knowledge in the careful and prudent application of treatments (Sadusk, 1963). Despite the malpractice overtones of iatrogenic illness (which might lead the profession to disguise rather than to disclose the problem), it has been the subject of extensive editorialization in medical journals (e.g., Kampmeier, 1966; McGrath, 1967) and systematic investigation (e.g., Moser, 1956, cites 144 studies while N. M. Scott, 1964, cites 203 studies).

Iatrogenic illness is recognized to be a not uncommon phenomenon. For example, Schimmel (1963) estimated that up to 20 per cent of the medical patients in one sample suffered from illnesses with iatrogenic complications. While it is not always easy to tell the difference between cases of iatrogenic complications of sound practice and complaints arising from malpractice, one can gain perspective on the size of the problem by realizing that approximately 193,000 cases of malpractice were brought to trial in the United States during the period of 1794-1955 (Shindell, 1965). If it is assumed, as is very reasonable, that only a small portion of the cases in which malpractice occurred were brought to trial, one can see that the problem is indeed serious.

Some of the conditions associated with iatrogenic illness in medical practice are summarized in Table 1. A review of the categories will reveal that willful wrongdoing is nowhere implied. Instead, each of the eight conditions can be viewed as a by-product of a serious attempt to offer sound medical treatment. Where the term "malpractice" is used, the implication is that the patient was exposed to diagnostic or therapeutic efforts which were offered with less skill than could have been expected.

Some of the consequences of iatrogenic illness are more serious than others. One recent investigation (Schimmel, 1964) demonstrated that in an institution where the average medical patient stayed for 11.4 days, those suffering from iatrogenic illnesses remained for an average of 28.7 days. Nor was iatrogenic illness a rare occurrence, as 240 incidences

TABLE 1

Conditions Associated with Iatrogenic Illness in Medicine

MAJOR CATEGORY	SUBCATEGORY	ILLUSTRATION
Consequences of Correct Practice	Correct diagnosis-wrong treatment	Varicose veins were correctly diagnosed but unnecessary surgery was performed in 203 cases (Rivin, 1966).
	Side effects of correct treatment	Complications from intravenous catheterization through umbil vein and complications from the treatment of respiratory distress syndrome are discussed (J. M. Scott, 1965).
	Side effects of correct drugs	Toxic drug reactions are encountered in 5-10% of patients due to interaction effects of multiple drugs, etc. (Side Effects, 1965).
		Effects of using drugs which are not thoroughly tested may be serious (Modell, 1963).
		Side effect of thiazide and potassium chloride may be ulceration of small intestine (Iatrogenic Ulcers, 1964).
		Disturbances attributable to cell injury, deficiency or imbalance in essential materials and developmental or genetic disturbances, etc., may result from use of certain drugs (Modell, 1965).
	Side effects of doctor-patient interaction	Eighteen of 476 cases of infertility were related to inter-action or diagnostic testing effects (Guerrero, 1966).
		Neurotic reactions may result from exaggeration of small cues from physician, etc. (Wahl, 1962).
		Neglect of social-psychological problems, etc., relate to iatrogenic illness (Ishikawa, Ohtsuka & Aoki, 1966).
		Patient committed suicide after hearing poor statement of

Consequences of Malpractice		
	Misdiagnosis	Surgery performed despite lack of supporting evidence (Lieberman, 1967). Misdiagnosis of heart disease from electrocardiographic reports, misinterpretation of laboratory results, and ill-considered investigations are all associated with iatrogenic illness (Lapinsky, 1964).
	Results of incorrect treatment or of correct treatment poorly performed	A study of 925 splenectomies found 244 (26%) probably due to incidental damage associated with other operations, although not all of these were upper abdominal operations (Rich, Lindner & Matthewson, 1967). Physicians may use outmoded treatment (Fisher, 1966). Cardiac surgical complications may result from malposition on the operating table, spinal manipulation, etc. (Miller, 1964).
	Side effects of incorrect drug	Gastroenteritis can result from alkalosis due to sodium bicarbonate which might be counterindicated (Brown, 1965).
	Consequences of impure instruments	Forty-one cases of viral hepatitis, resulting in 15 deaths, occurred when one physician used contaminated infusion tubes (Dougherty & Altman, 1963). Bacteriuria resulted following catheterization during surgery (Hodari & Hodgkinson, 1966).

were noted in 194 of the 1,014 patients admitted during the period of study.

Demographic studies in England and America show that iatrogenic illness is also a discernible cause of death. For example, 162 deaths were attributed to "therapeutic misadventure" in England and Wales during 1962 (Therapeutic Misadventure, 1965), while six such deaths per million population in America were found in 1960 (Burgess & Burgess, 1966). Because of the extent and gravity of the problem, the medical profession carries on a constant vigil to detect sources of and controls for the problems of iatrogenic illness.

Iatrogenic Illness as a Consequence of Psychiatric Treatment

There is far less literature on the iatrogenic factors in psychiatric treatment than is found in the literature on medical treatment and diagnosis. This may be a result of comparatively greater difficulty experienced by psychiatry in establishing causality, in formulating reasonably valid prognoses or even in substantiating the very existence of a mental illness. On the other hand, the reticence of psychiatrists to deal with this problem has been pointed out by at least one author (Chapman, 1964), who suggested that psychiatrists who advocate the virtues of their treatment with evangelical zeal are more likely to throw diagnoses at their critics than to take criticism seriously. In other situations, those who seek to study psychiatric malpractice may be denied access to the necessary data. As an illustration, one investigator (Bloom, 1967) sought to identify the factors associated with suicides at a mental institution only to find that necessary records were lost and relevant personnel unavailable.

Conditions associated with the incidence of iatrogenic

illness in psychiatry are summarized in Table 2. These conditions essentially parallel those identified in medicine, with the one exception that side effects of the doctor-patient interaction are included under the heading "Results of Incorrect Therapeutic Practice" because many writers place central importance upon "relationship" in psychotherapy (Gardner, 1964).

The incidence of malpractice in psychiatry has been blamed on faulty examination and commitment procedures (Morse, 1967), harmful consequences of physical and non-physical treatments, and failure to restrain a patient where restraint was a clear necessity (Bellamy, 1965). The consequences of iatrogenic illness and malpractice in psychiatry may be prolonged incapacitation or death, as will be pointed out in detail in succeeding chapters.

Summary

The decisions about which treatment to offer depend as much upon the persuasions of the therapist as they do upon the data presented by the patient. Therapists looking for intra-psychic difficulties will identify and treat such problems, while therapists concerned with behavioral functioning will locate and treat problems at the behavioral level. The choice of one treatment as opposed to another is hardly a matter of academics for the patient. Certain treatments expose him to the possibility of positive change while other treatments expose him to the risks of no change or negative change. The latter two possibilities do not receive the same amount of attention in psychiatry and psychotherapy as they receive in medicine in general. As a result, it is possible that the data-oriented self-corrective processes which are essential to the scientific character of psychotherapy may not be encouraged, so that faulty and inadequate treatment methods will improve little with the passage of time.

TABLE 2

Conditions Associated with Iatrogenic
Illness in Psychiatry

CATEGORY	ILLUSTRATION
Misdiagnosis	A patient was diagnosed as a schizophrenic, paranoid type when the actual problem was the patient's use of amphetamine sulfate (McDonald, 1964).
Results of Incorrect Therapeutic Practice	Three patients were unnecessarily hospitalized during treatment which instructed one to "get out aggressiveness," leading to destruction of his home; another to "remove sexual inhibitions," leading to promiscuity; and the last to end exploitation by his employer, leading to unemployment (Schmideberg, 1963). Psychodynamic treatment uncovered problems which patient could not handle, leading to exacerbation of presenting complaint (Von Wowern, 1966).
Side Effects of Drugs	Psychoactive drugs may lead to alteration of consciousness, fits, amnesia, paroxysmal headaches and hypertension attacks, extra-pyramidal syndromes (similar to Parkinson's disease), neuropathy-like syndromes, etc. (Skottowe, 1964). Brain disorders may result from certain drugs such as Tofranil, Thorazine or Elairl (Kane, 1965). Allergy and toxicity reactions to certain psychoactive drugs can affect all levels of the nervous system (Spillane, 1964).

Subsequent chapters of this book will present data which substantiate the possibility of failure and deterioration as a consequence of psychiatric hospitalization and psychotherapy, relating these failures to the faulty diagnostic process which is oriented to the identification of inner states. Following a detailed illustration of the pernicious effects of this iatrogenic process in the case of a young boy, an alternative, behavioral assessment framework will be proposed.

References

Baker, B. L. Symptom treatment and symptom substitution in enuresis. Paper presented at the annual meeting of the Association for Advancement of the Behavioral Therapies, Washington, D.C., September 1967.

Bellamy, W. Malpractice in psychiatry. *Diseases of the Nervous System,* 1965, 26, 312-320.

Bergin, A. E. Some implications of psychotherapy research to therapeutic practice. *Journal of Abnormal Psychology,* 1966, 71, 235-246.

Bloom, V. An analysis of suicide at a training center. *American Journal of Psychiatry,* 1967, 123, 918-925.

Bookbinder, L. J. Simple conditioning vs. the dynamic approach to symptoms and symptom substitution: A reply to Yates. *Psychological Reports,* 1962, 10, 71-77.

Breger, L. & McGaugh, J. L. Critique and reformulation of "learning theory" approaches to psychotherapy and neurosis. *Psychological Bulletin,* 1965, 63, 338-358.

Brown, J. Iatrogenic alkalosis in childhood. *Medical Journal of Australia,* 1965, 2, 3708-3709.

Bruck, M. Behavior modification theory and practice: A critical review. *Social Work,* 1968, 13(2), 43-55.

Burgess, A. M. & Burgess, A. M., Jr. Caring for the patient: A thrice-told tale. *New England Journal of Medicine,* 1966, 274, 241-244.

Cahoon, D. D. Symptom substitution and the behavior therapies: A reappraisal. *Psychological Bulletin,* 1968, 69, 149-156.

Carter, R. D. & Stuart, R. B. Behavior modification theory and practice, part I: A reply. *Social Work,* in press.

Chapman, A. H. Iatrogenic problems in psychotherapy. *Psychiatry Digest,* 1964, 25, 23-29.

Dougherty, W. J. & Altman, R. A physician related outbreak of hepatitis. *American Journal of Public Health,* 1963, 53, 1618-1622.

Fisher, T. L. Outmoded treatment. *Canadian Medical Association Journal,* 1966, 95, 630.

Gardner, G. G. The psychotherapeutic relationship. *Psychological Bulletin,* 1964, 61, 426-437.

Greenson, R. R. The classic psychoanalytic approach. In S. Arieti (Ed.),
  American handbook of psychiatry, Vol. 2. New York: Basic Books, 1959.
  Pp. 1399-1416.

Guerrero, C. D. Psychosomatic iatrogenic infertility. *Pacific Medicine and
  Surgery,* 1966, 74(3), 123-126.

Hodari, A. A. & Hodgkinson, C. P. Iatrogenic bateriuria and gynecologic surgery.
  American Journal of Obstetrics and Gynecology, 1966, 95, 153-164.

Iatrogenic ulcers of the small intestine. *British Medical Journal,* 1964, 5425,
  1611-1612.

Ishikawa, H., Ohtsuka, H. & Aoki, M. Iatrogenic disease in general medicine.
  Psychosomatics, 1966, 7(3), 131-138.

Kampmeier, R. H. Diseases of medical progress. *Southern Medical Journal,* 1966,
  59, 871-872.

Kane, F. J. & Ewing, J. A. Iatrogenic brain syndrome. *Southern Medical Journal,*
  1965, 58, 875-877.

Kanfer, F. H. & Saslow, G. Behavioral diagnosis. In C. Franks (Ed.), *Assessment
  and status of the behavior therapies and associated developments.* New
  York: McGraw-Hill, in press.

Lapinsky, G. B. The pathogenesis and prevention of iatrogenic illness. *South
  African Medical Journal,* 1964, 38, 52-56.

Lieberman, A. The case of iatrogenic idiopathy. *Journal of the Indiana State
  Medical Association,* 1967, 60, 1049-1052.

McConnell, J. V. Psychoanalysis must go. *Esquire,* 1968, 70(4), 176ff.

McDonald, R. L. Iatrogenic amphetamine psychosis. *Americal Journal of
  Psychiatry,* 1964, 120, 1200-1201.

McGrath, W. B. Iatrogenics, with a grain of salt. *Arizona Medicine,* 1967, 24,
  731.

Miller, H. Iatrogenic neurological diseases: Some neurological complications of
  surgical treatment. *Proceedings of the Royal Society of Medicine,* 1964,
  57, 143-146.

Modell, W. Hazards of new drugs. *Science,* 1963, 139, 1180-1185.

Modell, W. Drug-induced diseases. *Annual Review of Pharmacology,* 1965,
  5, 285-304.

Morse, H. N. Psychiatric responsibility and tort liability. *Journal of Forensic
  Science,* 1967, 12, 305-358.

Moser, R. Diseases of medical progress. *New England Journal of Medicine,* 1956,
  255, 606-614.

Paul, G. L. *Insight vs. desensitization in psychotherapy.* Stanford, Calif.:
  Stanford University Press, 1966.

Rich, N. M., Lindner, H. H. & Matthewson, C. Splenectomy incidental to iatrogenic trauma. *American Journal of Surgery,* 1967, 110, 209-217.

Rivin, S. Recurrent varicose veins. *Medical Journal of Australia,* 1966, 1,
  1097-1102.

Sadusk, J. Medical malpractice: 1. Causes. *Connecticut Medicine,* 1963, 27,
  614-619.

Scheflen, A. E. Analysis of the thought model which persists in psychiatry.
  Psychosomatic Medicine, 1958, 20, 235-241.

Schimmel, E. The physician as pathogen. *Journal of Chronic Diseases,* 1963, 16, 1-4.

Schimmel, E. The hazards of hospitalization. *Annals of Internal Medicine,* 1964, 60, 100-110.

Schmideberg, M. Iatrogenic disturbance. *American Journal of Psychiatry,* 1963, 119, 899.

Scott, J. M. Iatrogenic lesions in babies following umbilical cord catheterization. *Archives of Disease in Childhood,* 1965, 40, 426-429.

Scott, N. M., Jr. Gastrointestinal diseases of medical progress. *New York Medical Journal,* 1964, 64, 607-618.

Shindell, S. A survey of the law of medical practice: IV. Negligence in the practice of medicine. *Journal of the American Medical Association,* 1965, 194, 281-287.

Side effects of drugs. *The Lancet,* 1965, 1, 308-309.

Skottowe, I. Iatrogenic neurological diseases: Neurological complications of psychiatric treatment. *Proceedings of the Royal Society of Medicine,* 1964, 57, 140-143.

Spiegel, H. Is symptom removal dangerous? *American Journal of Psychiatry,* 1967, 10, 1279-1282.

Spillane, J. D. Iatrogenic neurological diseases: Drug-induced neurological disorders. *Proceedings of the Royal Society of Medicine,* 1964, 57, 135-140.

Stuart, R. B. Guide to the planning and evaluation of behavior modification. Unpublished manuscript, University of Michigan, 1968.

Therapeutic misadventure. *British Medical Journal,* 1965, 5444, 1205-1206.

Turner, R. J. & Cumming, J. Theoretical malaise and community mental health. In E. L. Cowen, E. A. Gardner & M. Zax (Eds.), *Emergent approaches to mental health problems.* New York: Appleton-Century-Crofts, 1967. Pp. 40-62.

Ullmann, L. P. & Krasner, L. Introduction. In L. P. Ullmann & L. Krasner (Eds.), *Case studies in behavior modification.* New York: Holt, Rinehart & Winston, 1965. Pp. 1-64.

Von Wowern, F. Iatrogenesis: Sensation of disease and aggravation of pre-existing disease, produced by doctors. *Psychiatria et Neurologia,* 1966, 151, 46-53.

Wahl, C. W. Iatrogenic neuroses, their production and prevention. *Psychosomatics,* 1962, 3, 450-453.

Whitehead, A. N. *Science and the modern world.* New York: Macmillan, 1925.

Wiest, W. M. Some recent criticisms of behaviorism and learning theory. *Psychological Bulletin,* 1967, 67, 214-225.

Wolpe, J. *Psychotherapy by reciprocal inhibition.* Stanford, Calif.: Stanford University Press, 1958.

Yates, A. J. Symptoms and symptom substitution. *Psychological Review,* 1958, 65, 371-374.

2
Failure and Deterioration Associated with Psychiatric Hospitalization

On any day of 1966, over 525,000 patients resided in federal, state, county and private mental hospitals (Bureau of the Census, 1968, p. 74). With over 325,000 admissions and discharges in 1966, approximately 800,000 different individuals spent some time in mental institutions oriented to long-term care. When patients enter mental institutions, they do so with the justifiable expectation that they will be relieved from the distress of their "mental illness." Accordingly they expect that scientifically validated treatments will be used by trained professionals operating in therapeutic environments which have been carefully engineered to maximize the probability of successful outcomes. The surroundings reinforce patients in this expectation. The personnel have medical job titles, the institution is called a "hospital," professionalized routines are maintained and patient behavior is talked about in scientific language. Unfortunately, the promise of such scientific treatment is frequently not fulfilled.

Outcome of Hospitalization

Because "mental illness" is an indefinite phenomenon, it is difficult to determine degrees of change, let alone the absolute presence or absence of an illness. Therefore, in evaluating the effects of hospitalization, two very crude sets of criteria are used. The first set concerns whether or not the patient is discharged and succeeds in remaining outside of the hospital following his release. The second set concerns measurement of the degree of successful adjustment to family and occupational responsibilities, on the one hand, and measurement of the degree of symptomatology, on the other.

Studies conducted as long as five centuries ago used the first criterion. Ullmann (1967) has reviewed considerable evidence of early treatments showing that from 60 to 90 per cent of all hospitalized patients were successfully discharged to the community (see also Arlidge, 1859; Bockoven, 1963; Dain, 1964; Dunham & Weinberg, 1960; Hunter & Macalpine, 1963; Jones & Sidebotham, 1962; Solomon, 1957). Today, approximately half of the newly admitted mental patients will be discharged during the first two years of their institutionalization, an additional 25 per cent will be discharged between the second and fourth year, and the probability of discharge is virtually nil for those remaining longer than four years (Ellsworth, Mean & Clayton, 1958; Kramer, Goldstein, Israel & Johnson, 1956; Vitale, 1962).

Even if the patient is successful in winning his discharge from an institution, however, his chances of remaining in the community may not be great. The results of several studies support this unhappy conclusion: (a) as many as half of the 325,000 annual admissions to mental hospitals are readmissions (Silverstein, 1968); (b) as many as 40 per cent of patients offered intensive short-term treatment remain in the hospital or are rehospitalized within six months of the termination of treatment (Dinitz, Lefton, Angrist & Pasamanick, 1961); (c) children who have been hospitalized are likely to be rehospitalized as adults for the same complaints (Pritchard & Graham, 1966); and (d) patients receiving special treatments such as insulin coma, ECT, electronarcosis, lobotomy or psychotherapy did not outperform patients who received only hospital routine as therapy (Appel, Meyers & Scheflen, 1953).

Above and beyond the failure of patients to leave hospitals or their failure to remain in the community following discharge, considerable evidence suggests that patients either do not change in hospitals or such changes do not persist when they return to the community. Of seven studies in this area, only one showed positive changes in patient behavior, and this study was based upon social worker ratings rather than upon self-evaluations of the patient or assessments by his relatives (Lewinsohn & Nichols, 1964). Three studies found little or no change in work patterns following hospitalization (Bockoven, Pandiscio & Solomon, 1956; Ellsworth, Foster, Childers, Arthur & Kroeker, 1968; McPartland & Richart, 1966), while two studies showed virtually no change in the areas of self-care and social behavior (Berger, Rice, Sewall & Lemkau, 1963; Gurel, 1967). A final study demonstrated that even following intensive treatment, patient behavior fell below the modest objectives of meeting minimum standards of behavior acceptable in the community (Stimpert, Sinnett & Wilkens, 1966).

While the increasing rates of failure of hospitalization may be discouraging, the rate of deterioration during hospitalization is even more alarming. The most negative finding concerns the higher death rates among mental patients. One study in England, for example, found that:

> The mortality in the present sample was much higher than in the general population of Greater London. With due allowance for differences in the age structure of the mental hospital and general populations, the mortality among male patients during the first 3½ years of mental hospital life was found to be 9 times and among female patients 6 times that of the general population. In the first year of hospital life the excess mortality of the patient population was even higher, being 13 times greater for male and 8 times greater for female patients than the corresponding sections of the Greater London population [Norris, 1959, p. 264].

Many of the patients died during the first few days of hospitalization, but with this group discounted there is still a clear-cut increase in the probability of death following admission to at least some psychiatric institutions.

Patients fortunate enough to physically survive hospitalization have the additional risk of behavioral deterioration. The typical study in this area measures the rate of patient "symptomatology" prior to admission, during critical periods of the hospitalization, and following discharge from the hospital. One study of 143 male veteran psychiatric patients found that "psychiatric hospitalization operates to intensify feelings of decline and impotence and to release sexual and aggressive impulses [Mahrer, 1963, p. 266]," while other studies found an increase in more typical psychiatric symptomatology (Johnston & McNeal, 1965; Mahrer & Mason, 1965; Masserman & Carmichael, 1938).

However, there is some evidence that these deterioration effects may be confined to certain patients receiving certain treatments. In point of fact, it is probably always essential to specify types of therapists, patients and settings in evaluating research pertaining to the effectiveness of any intervention techniques. For example, one study (Fairweather, Simon, Gebhard, Weingarten, Holland, Sanders, Stone & Reahl, 1960) showed that two groups of inpatients benefited from psychotherapy while long-term psychotics deteriorated during its course. A particularly alarming finding of this study is that long-term psychotic controls showed a large positive change during the same period. In other words, certain types of patients who did not receive this particular therapy fared better than patients who did receive such treatment.

In reviewing this evidence, it can be concluded that commitment to psychiatric hospitalization is not without considerable risk. While perhaps as many as half of the patients so treated are successful in achieving lasting discharge from the institution, a sizable number fails to be discharged, undergoes additional behavioral difficulty or suffers from the increased danger of physical illness. There are several explanations for these negative therapeutic results, including limitations in the theory of treatment, antitherapeutic aspects of hospital organization and non-patient-oriented bases of decision-making. Each of these will be explored below.

Theories of Institutional Treatment

The type of hospital treatment offered to the "mentally ill" person has naturally varied as a consequence of evolving theories of mental illness. A very brief review of these theories may shed light upon the current situation and place into context the recommendations that follow.

The early Greeks recognized that mental illness resulted from social experience and therefore sought to cure it through change in the social environment. By the onset of the Dark Ages, throughout the Middle Ages, and among many mental health professionals today, the causes and phenomena of mental illness are ascribed to factors within the individual. During the Dark Ages, the demon theory was at its peak and treatments consisted of cruel means of exorcism in an effort to purge the sufferer of his possessor. According to Deutsch (1949), the physicians of the later Middle Ages and the Puritan Age set the causes of mental illness in organic processes, particularly in lesions of the brain, while Bockoven (1957) cites a closely parallel religious view that the mentally ill person had succumbed to "animal instincts." Both points of view accepted the notion that the mentally ill were insensitive to pain, cold and discomfort, so physical care was totally neglected and cruel attempts were made to establish sensory contact, or to punish animal instincts to gain control of them.

In this tradition, Dr. Benjamin Rush, known as the "father of American psychiatry," developed his tranquilizing chair, which restricted all movement for long periods of time, and his energizing board, which spun at high velocity with the patient strapped to it head down so the blood would flow to his head. As another example, the famous Pennsylvania Hospital reported treatments such as the following:

> Their scalps were shaved and blistered. They were bled to the point of syncope; purged until the alimentary canal failed to yield anything but mucus, and in the intervals they were chained by the waist or ankle to the cell wall [Deutsch, 1949, p. 80].

In a review of mental hospital care 20 years ago, Deutsch (1948) noted that many cruel practices were still used, although without exorcism or rites. The chains were used; water treatments were used in the form of tubs in which patients not infrequently thought they were being drowned; narcosis was used; lobotomies represented the technical triumph; and ECT was regarded as therapeutically effective because of its resemblance to death agonies. While these treatments have undoubtedly vanished from even the most primitive hospitals, they have been replaced in many places by overdoses of medication and social isolation coupled with inactivity.

While cruel practices of mental-patient care continued, a second trend toward more humanitarian approaches was developing. Spurred by the French Revolution and its spirit of questioning and respect for the individual, Pinel took the chains from the patients at Bicetre Asylum in 1792 and, along with Chiarugi in Italy and Tuke in England, led the way toward relative enlightenment in mental-patient care. The program which emerged from the reform was termed "moral treatment" by Bockoven (1957), who wrote of it as follows:

> The word 'moral' as it was used then conveyed both the idea that insane individuals be treated in accordance with their moral rights as individuals, and the idea that the treatment revealed to the patient the moral of his life story in relation to other people. The fact that the hospital chaplain worked in partnership with the physician in treating patients suggests that mental illness was regarded as something of a moral problem in the religious sense [p. 522].

Bockoven thus asserts a practical connection between the dominant contemporary view of mental illness and religion, offering additional confirmation for the belief that religious views (the Protestant ethic) play a dominant role in current mental health ideology.

Moral treatment proceeded slowly in America, slowed by at least two factors. The American Association of Medical Superintendents (heads of asylums) was formed in order to argue against permissiveness and for the use of mechanical restraints. In addition, moral treatment was inadvertently slowed by Dorothea Linde Dix's crusade for separate institutions for the mentally ill. Miss Dix's efforts were so successful that huge numbers of patients flowed into institutional settings that were without a technology for their care. Nevertheless, the moral treatment concept survived to spirit today's notion of a "therapeutic milieu."

Typical writings about the therapeutic milieu make few, if any, assumptions about the etiology of mental disorder (e.g., Schwartz, 1957). Typically its proponents call for a milieu which will:

(1) Provide the patient with experiences that will minimize his distortions of reality; (2) facilitate his realistic and meaningful communicative exchange with others; (3) facilitate his participation with others so that he derives greater satisfaction and security therefrom; (4) reduce his anxiety and increase his comfort; (5) increase his self-esteem; (6) provide him with insight into the causes and manifestations of his mental illness; (7) mobilize his initiative and motivate him to realize more fully his potentialities for creativity and productiveness [Schwartz, 1957, p. 131].

The basic therapeutic postulate is apparently an insight-producing developmental experience which should result in more effective social behavior. Unfortunately, the specific techniques of milieu management are elusive and there is very little, if any, research data which can be offered in support of its effectiveness. Furthermore, it can be criticized from several points of view. The most important criticism is that the environment to which the patient is expected to adjust in treatment is so alien from the environment outside the hospital that success within the institution bears little relationship to effective adjustment in the community (Rapoport, Rapoport & Rosow, 1960). A second criticism is that the milieu concept usually allows the patient to receive many positive rewards which are not contingent on adaptive behaviors. Also, the patient bears no responsibility for maladaptive behaviors. To the extent that human learning depends upon feedback about both positive and negative responses, the milieu approach denies its patients access to important variables in changing behavior.

At the present time it must be concluded that the therapeutic milieu has an appealing rhetoric but little technology. To the extent that the therapeutic milieu is a general ideology in mental institutions, these settings must be viewed as lacking in technology. This is, in fact, the conclusion of Perrow's (1965) trenchant analysis of the organization of mental hospitals. Clearly, while some more promising programs exist for the development of a more effective program of hospitalization (Ayllon & Azrin, 1968), the vast majority of hospital programs today are frankly incapable of fulfilling their charge. This was, in fact, the bleak conclusion reached by one observer only a few years ago:

> One is reluctantly forced to admit that we simply do not possess the factual knowledge as of 1957 which permits us to say that we have any treatment procedure in psychiatry which promises a better outlook for a particular illness than does nature left to her own devices [Hastings, 1958, p. 1057].

Organizational Factors Contributing to Hospital Treatment Failures

While it may be a naive assumption, it would seem that one requirement of an effective therapeutic environment is that it must stimulate a high level of appropriate social behavior. In fact, however, hospital environments have been shown to have exactly the reverse effect. This effect has been termed "prison stupor" (Meyerson, 1939; Strassman, Thaler & Schein, 1956) and is characterized by a general lack of interest in self-care, a general withdrawal from social contact and a general decrement in activity level. While it might be claimed that this withdrawal pattern is endemic to the pre-morbid behavior of the mental patient, at least one observer has shown that withdrawal by hospitalized children begins at the time of hospitalization:

> . . . *acute withdrawal* begins with the moment the child enters the hospital. There is a sudden dramatic decline in general interests and participation in peer activities. Frequently, we find dramatic symptoms, like negativism, command automatism, mutism, refusal of food, etc. Spells of bizarre posturizing, resembling catatonia, are encountered. Intellectual activities may come to all but a standstill, and meaningful communication is sometimes impossible [von Brauchitsch, 1965, p. 14].

Prison stupor is undoubtedly a consequence of the "mor-tification" (Goffman, 1961) of the mental patient, as he is stripped of the supports of individuality and coerced into acceptance of hospital routine (Barton, 1959; Bockoven, 1963; Dunham & Weinberg, 1960; Sommer & Osmond, 1961). Patients are often required to give up their personal clothing and accept hospital garb; they do not generally have access to places to keep personal belongings and therefore commonly see personal possessions lost or stolen; they are required to sleep, eat, relax and toilet in public surroundings; and they are required to live according to hospital rather than personally meaningful routines.

In addition to losing individuality as a natural consequence of life in a total institution, mental patients are also denied contact with interested family members, which means they must live without the natural consequences of important classes of socially assertive or competitive behavior, and the rate of these behaviors falls as a result. Furthermore, when the patient is absent, those family routines which involved the patient are interrupted (Mendel, 1966a) and the family naturally further disengages itself from the patient, thereby furthering his isolation.

Denied the necessary supports of the routines of his pre-institutional life, the patient is vulnerable to the influence of hospital staff. In most institutional settings the meaningful staff group is the attendants (Belknap, 1956, p. 65), since the patient has by far the greatest amount of contact with personnel in this echelon. The attendants as a group are generally poorly paid, overworked and untrained. Their natural goal is to promote patient acceptance of hospital routine, which implies a pattern of passivity and withdrawal (Bloom, 1963; Lehrman, 1961), which in turn leads to a profound dependency (Vitale, 1962). The dependency is a consequence of the patient's position within the institutional structure; he depends upon the attendant's approval for his food, recreation, medication—for every aspect of his comfort. Unfortunately, "custodialism" can be said to characterize the behavior of the attendants (Belknap, 1956; Brown & Ishiyama, 1965; Greenblatt, Levinson & Williams, 1957), and hospital ward staff may be more oriented toward achieving "the quiet day" than toward promoting more effective patient care. In fact, Ullmann (1967) has suggested that aides tend to make decisions oriented to "the goal of . . . the comfort of the aide and not the ultimate adjustment of the patient [p. 25]."

When staff does interact with patients, there is some evidence that the interactions are commonly to the patient's disadvantage. It can be shown, for example, that the staff uses its important influence—the control of privileges such as grounds passes, etc.— (Longabaugh, Eldred, Bell & Sherman, 1966) to promote pathological behaviors (Buehler, Patterson & Furness, 1966; Christ & Wagner, 1966; Lovaas, Freitag, Gold & Kassorka, 1965). When staff has little time to spend with patients and when this time is spent following negative rather than positive behaviors, it is clear that the staff works, however inadvertently, toward reinforcement of problematic behaviors. Indeed, one of the most inescapable impressions drawn from visits to psychiatric wards is the relative neglect of patients engaging in such social activities as quiet conversation or card games, and the almost total staff involvement with the patient believed to be "acting out." In this manner, inappropriate behaviors are reinforced with attention while acceptable behaviors are extinguished through inattention (Schwartz & Shockley, 1956). Paradoxically enough, one careful study (Gelfand, Gelfand & Dobson, 1967) demonstrated that if the prototype of effective therapist-patient interaction is the reinforcement of positive behavior and the neglect of negative behavior, then patients have been shown to be better therapists than the professional staff.

Finally, it should be noted that staff shortages may further complicate the general problems of patient-staff interaction. While Albee (1967) has suggested that shortages of mental health personnel may have already passed the critical level, Silverstein (1968, pp. 143-148) presents specific data showing that in 1964 the state hospitals in Pennsylvania lacked 30 per cent of the required psychiatrists, 38 per cent of the required psychologists, 61 per cent of the required nurses, 68 per cent of the required social workers, and 17 per cent of the required attendants. Curiously enough, the only staff category which did not report vacancies was that designated "Other 'Activities' Personnel." In a similar vein, Kubie (1968a) has noted that there are only 20,000 psychiatrists in America, many of whom spend time in private practice, administration, research and teaching—leaving only a small number to treat the estimated 800,000 hospitalized mental patients. In view of these shortages it is not surprising that staff must orient itself to post hoc efforts to deal with disturbances rather than to the promotion of constructive programs.

In summary, it can be said that there are characteristic organizational patterns in mental hospitals which contribute to patient failures, whatever their relationship to therapeutic successes. When patients are denied access to the stimuli that maintain adaptive functioning and when they are instead subjected to environments that suppress rather than encourage assertive behavior, the stage is set for patterns of withdrawal. These patterns are further reinforced by ordinary patient-staff interactions which reward problematic behaviors with attention and extinguish acceptable behaviors through inattention.

Patterns of Decision-Making in Hospitals

Ideally, decisions pertaining to the course of treatment offered to patients during hospitalization should be based upon a careful assessment of patient need. Unfortunately, this may not be the case in many instances. First, hospital protocol may have as much to do with the details of the patient's career as any other factor. It was shown, for example, that patients in one New York state hospital had an average length of stay one third as long as patients in another, comparable hospital in the state (Cattell & Forster, 1964). The same effect can be seen among institutions in different states. For example, in 1965 when the populations of New York and California were almost equal, New York had a daily average of mental hospital in-patients approximating 88,000, while California had approximately 33,000 in-patients (Bureau of the Census, 1969, pp. 12 and 75). Second, staff idiosyncrasy may have an equally profound effect upon the decisions made about patient care. For example, Mendel (1967) has shown that as residents moved from the first to the fourth week of training, the rate of drugs prescribed by the residents fell from 70 to 20 per cent, and if this training occurred during the first three months of their residency year they were 24 per cent more likely to prescribe drugs than if the training took place during the last three months of that year.

In a second, even more revealing study, Mendel and Rapport (1968) reviewed the decisions of 32 clinicians to hospitalize 269 patients. They found, among other things, that: (a) social workers tended to hospitalize fewer patients than did psychiatrists or psychologists; (b) the decision to hospitalize was more closely related to previous history of hospitalization than to the severity of symptoms presented at the time the decision was made; (c) patients seen during evenings and weekends were more than twice as likely to be hospitalized as patients seen during the normal work day; and (d) the clinicians were unaware of the criteria which they themselves used:

All 32 decision makers reported on the follow-up questionnaire that they thought the severity of symptoms of the patient was a major factor in their decision for or against hospitalization [while] none of the decision makers felt that his decision for or against hospitalization was influenced by the history of previous hospitalization [p. 11].

A third factor contributing to decisions about patients has been shown to be institutional convenience. Cumming and Cumming (1957) have suggested that the decision to discharge a patient may have more to do with "how badly his bed is needed [p. 68]" than with his "mental status." The patient's contribution to the maintenance of the hospital may also be a factor:

> Many patients work in the hospital industries, e. g., the laundry, the farm, the upholsterer's shop. Without this patient labor, the hospital could not operate on its tiny outlay per patient. The patient who is getting better is put to work; if he continues to improve, his work is valuable, and there is then set up a complicated strain toward keeping him in the hospital, cured of his psychosis, but soon too desocialized to go home [Cumming & Cumming, 1957, p. 55].

A fourth problem that obstructs effective decision-making about mental patients is inherent in the fact that the very definition of the illness of a particular patient is a consequence of his having been labeled a deviant by someone in his natural environment. Goffman (1961) has indicated that a dilemma confronts mental health personnel when they seek to make medical decisions about social problems:

> Ordinarily the pathology which first draws attention to the patient's condition is conduct that is 'inappropriate in the situation.' But the decision as to whether a given act is appropriate or inappropriate must often necessarily be a lay decision, simply because we have no technical mapping of the various behavioral subcultures in our society, let alone the standards of conduct prevailing in each of them. Diagnostic decisions, except for extreme symptoms, can become ethnocentric, the observer judging from his own culture's point of view individuals' conduct that can really be judged only

from the perspective of the group from which they derive. Further, since inappropriate behavior is typically behavior that someone does not like and finds extremely troublesome, decisions concerning it tend to be political, in the sense of expressing the special interests of some particular faction of person rather than interests that can be said to be above the concerns of any particular grouping, as in the case of physical pathology [pp. 363-364].

By the same token, careful research has shown (e.g., Freeman & Simmons, 1963) that family willingness to tolerate different forms of problematic behavior materially influences the feasibility and success of patient discharge to the community. For example, Fairweather and his associates (1964) found that patients treated with a most sophisticated treatment nevertheless returned to the hospital because the community would not accept them upon discharge. Therefore the designation of illness and cure appears to be a social rather than a medical problem and its delineation as a medical problem only contributes to a low level of effective decision-making.

This varied evidence at least partly supports the presumption that decisions which materially affect the life status of patients are based on criteria other than patient need. A *full* substantiation of this assumption would contribute forcefully to explaining the failure of hospital treatment or the deterioration of patient functioning following hospitalization.

Alternatives to Psychiatric Hospitalization

In view of the risks in psychiatric hospitalization, one may naturally wonder about the risks of not being hospitalized. All of the evidence reviewed by the author supports the view that at least *75 per cent of those persons hospitalized are not in need of hospitalization,* as determined by their ability to remain in the community following denial of hospitalization or treatment in hospitals for only very brief periods (Cooper & Early, 1961; Deiter, Hanford, Hummel & Lubach, 1965;

Herjanic & LaFave, 1966; Longnecker, Miller, Richardson & Willingham, 1968). In a study which must be regarded as a classic, Mendel (1966b) found that of 2,926 patients over the age of 18 who were admitted to the psychiatric ward of Los Angeles County General Hospital, 2,225 could be readily discharged to the community. Mendel studied these patients carefully in terms of community adjustment in light of their hospital treatment. He found that:

1) Seventy-five per cent of all patients [with] the diagnosis schizophrenia (2,926) admitted over a specified period can be discharged to the community.

2) The rate of discharge to the community does not vary significantly with the length of stay in the hospital.

3) The readmission rate of schizophrenic patients discharged to the community over a two-year period is 20.5 per cent. The rate of readmissions does not vary with the length of hospitalization during the index period.

4) The level of function during the two years of post-index hospitalization does not vary with the number of days of hospitalization in regard to such measures as further hospitalization, further treatment, or financial status. The post-hospital course *does vary* [italics mine] in regard to ability to function socially, at work and in the family. Function in these areas is statistically significantly related to the number of days of hospitalization. That is, the shorter the hospitalization, the higher the level of function in the post-hospital course.

5) Of the total number of patients rehospitalized in this study (20.5 per cent), the number of days of hospitalization during the two-year follow-up period varied significantly with the number of days of index hospitalization. The briefer the index of hospitalization, the fewer the number of days of subsequent hospitalization in the two-year follow-up period.

6) When 18 schizophrenic patients were discharged arbitrarily, the rate of return did not vary with the number of days of index hospitalization even during the first seven days of hospitalization [Mendel, 1966b, p. 230].

In view of these results and others which show an inverse relationship between patient improvement and the length of hospital stay, Mendel (1968) has concluded that:

... I am now ready to propose that the psychiatric hospital serves no unique or useful function in the treatment intervention of mental illness . . . I propose that mental illness is never well treated in a psychiatric hospital, that taking the patient into a psychiatric hospital further complicates the disorganization resulting from the mental illness and in no way prepares him to resume his life in the community [p. 245].

As alternatives to hospitalization, a variety of forms of community care are possible. Morrissey (1967) has shown the advantages of family care, Ellsworth (1968) has shown the advantages of foster care, McPartland (1964) has shown the advantages of day care, and Mendel (1968) has experimented with a variety of means of maintaining patients in the community, using extramural services. In light of these encouraging developments, it appears that programs drawing upon methods other than mental hospital care should be given serious consideration.

The Prospect of Change

Despite the fact that 175,000 of the 325,000 patients admitted to mental hospitals in America annually are readmissions (Silverstein, 1968), and despite the vast array of specific clinical reports which shed serious doubt upon the effectiveness of psychiatric hospitalization, these programs continue to expand. Stuart (1969) has offered several explanations for the failure of efforts to stem the tide of growth in the number and population of mental institutions, including: (1) the attempted use of individually focused clinical programs as an effort to contain the effects of problems of broad social dislocation which actually require much larger expenditures, (2) the use of hospitals merely to rid families of relatives whose behavior has been difficult to control or to aid communities in controlling deviance, and (3) a means of extending normative controls of behavior through the use of medico-scientific terminology.

The sad fact is that when changes in this system are proposed, they are commonly thwarted without adequate consideration. Discouraging evidence is available which sheds light upon some of the problems in promoting program change, such as very suppressive measures in institutional (Sanders, Smith & Weinman, 1967, p. 301ff) and community settings (Graziano, 1969). Nowhere is the situation better illustrated, however, than in an exchange between Klerman (1968), who set forth an empirically based argument favoring community care, and Kubie (1968a), who suggested that community care subjects patients to "relative isolation," and that "if imprecise concepts such as 'schizophrenia' are fed into a computer nothing can come out but additional errors to magnify those of the original programming [1968b, p. 450]." Kubie further threatened, however obliquely, that "new methods" might result in grave danger to the patient:

> The current use and misuse of tranquilizers afford many examples of how the elimination of symptoms can sometimes mask the inexorable advance of the process of disease, much as the excessive misuse of morphine in past decades would mask the symptoms of an acute appendix until it ruptured, to provide a fatal peritonitis. Psychiatry is not exempt from such risks [1968a, p. 422].

This is a pointed reference to the "medical model" which is often used as a basis for arguments against innovative treatments.

Summary

In summary, it can be said that patients can have a realistic expectation of modest gain from psychiatric hospitalization and at least a moderate expectation of deterioration. These outcomes can be explained by the facts that "there is no appropriate treatment technology available for the large public mental hospital [Perrow, 1965, p. 924];" various forces within the hospital militate against improvement and in fact promote deterioration; patients may be offered medical-psychiatric hospitalization for social problems; and many decisions are made on a less than rational basis. The severity of the problem has been aptly summarized by Dr. Hans von Brauchitsch (1966) in the following terms:

> ... the hospital seduces the socially and emotionally handicapped child to gravitate into the unchallenging world of the chronically insane, ... it reinforces rather than attenuates his morbid tendency to avoid competitive situations, and, by cutting the most important ties to the outside world of reality, invites him to freely adopt the prevalent models of mental illness as an appropriate way of life [p. 7].

References

Albee, G. W. The relation of conceptual models to manpower needs. In E. L. Cowen, E. A. Gardner & M. Zax (Eds.), *Emergent approaches to mental health problems.* New York: Appleton-Century-Crofts, 1967. Pp. 63-73.

Appel, K. E., Meyers, J. M. & Scheflen, A. E. Prognosis in psychiatry. *Archives of Neurology and Psychiatry,* 1953, 70, 459-468.

Arlidge, J. T. *On the state of lunacy and the legal provision for the insane, with observations on the construction and organization of asylums.* London: John Churchill, 1859.

Ayllon, T. & Azrin, N. *The token economy: A motivational system for therapy and rehabilitation.* New York: Appleton-Century-Crofts, 1968.

Barton, R. *Institutional neurosis.* Bristol, England: Wright, 1959.

Belknap, I. *Human problems of a state mental hospital.* New York: McGraw-Hill, 1956.

Berger, D. G., Rice, C. E., Sewall, L. G. & Lemkau, P. V. Factors affecting the adequacy of patient community adjustment information obtained from the community. *Mental Hygiene,* 1963, 47, 452-460.

Bloom, S. W. *The doctor and his patient.* New York: Russell Sage Foundation, 1963.

Bockoven, J. S. Some relationships between cultural attitudes toward individuality and care of the mentally ill: An historical study. In M. Greenblatt, D. J. Levinson & R. H. Williams (Eds.), *The patient and the mental hospital.* Glencoe, Ill.: Free Press, 1957. Pp. 517-526.

Bockoven, J. S. *Moral treatment in American psychiatry.* New York: Springer, 1963.

Bockoven, J. S., Pandiscio, A. R. & Solomon, H. C. Social adjustment of patients in the community three years after commitment to the Boston Psychopathic Hospital. *Mental Hygiene,* 1956, 40, 353-374.

Brown, A. F. & Ishiyama, T. The relationship of interpersonal values and patient success in a mental hospital. *Journal of Psychiatric Nursing,* 1965, 3, 208-219.

Buehler, R., Patterson, G. R. & Furness, J. The reinforcement of behavior in institutional settings. *Behaviour Research and Therapy,* 1966, 4, 157-167.

Bureau of the Census. *Statistical abstract of the United States.* Washington, D.C.: U. S. Government Printing Office, 1968.

Cattell, J. P. & Forster, E. Evaluation of patients following treatment in general hospital outpatient clinics. In P. H. Hoch & J. Zubin (Eds.), *The evaluation of psychiatric treatment.* New York: Grune & Stratton, 1964. Pp. 247-253.

Christ, A. E. & Wagner, N. N. Iatrogenic factors in residential treatment: A problem in staff training. *American Journal of Orthopsychiatry,* 1966, 36, 725-729.

Cooper, A. B. & Early, D. F. Evolution in the mental hospital: Review of a hospital population. *British Medical Journal,* 1961, 1, 1600-1603.

Cumming, J. & Cumming, E. Social equilibrium and social change in the large mental hospital. In M. Greenblatt, D. J. Levinson & R. H. Williams (Eds.), *The patient and the mental hospital.* Glencoe, Ill.: Free Press, 1957. Pp. 50-72.

Dain, N. *Concepts of insanity in the United States, 1789-1865.* New Brunswick, N. J.: Rutgers University Press, 1964.

Deiter, J. B., Hanford, D. B., Hummel, R. T. & Lubach, J. E. Brief in-patient treatment—a pilot study. *Mental Hospitals,* 1965, 16, 95-98.

Deutsch, A. *The shame of the states.* New York: Harcourt, Brace & World, 1948.

Deutsch, A. *The mentally ill in America.* New York: Columbia University Press, 1949.

Dinitz, S., Lefton, M., Angrist, S. & Pasamanick, B. Psychiatric and social attributes as predictors of case outcome in mental hospitalization. *Social Problems,* 1961, 8, 322-328.

Dunham, H. W. & Weinberg, S. K. *The culture of the state mental hospital.* Detroit: Wayne State University Press, 1960.

Ellsworth, R. B., Foster, L., Childers, B., Arthur, G. & Kroeker, D. Hospital and community adjustment as perceived by psychiatric patients, their families, and staff. *Journal of Consulting and Clinical Psychology,* 1968, 52 (5, Part 2).

Ellsworth, R. B., Mead, B. T. & Clayton, W. H. The rehabilitation and disposition of chronically hospitalized schizophrenic patients. *Mental Hygiene,* 1958, 42, 343-348.

Fairweather, G. W. (Ed.) *Social psychology in treating mental illness: An experimental approach.* New York: Wiley, 1964.

Fairweather, G. W., Simon, R., Gebhard, M. E., Weingarten, E., Holland, J. L., Sanders, R., Stone, G. B. & Reahl, J. E. Relative effectiveness of psychotherapeutic programs: A multi-criteria comparison of four programs for three different patient groups. *Psychological Monographs,* 1960, 74 (5, Whole No. 492).

Freeman, H. E. & Simmons, O. G. *The mental patient comes home.* New York: Wiley, 1963.

Gelfand, D. M., Gelfand, S. & Dobson, W. R. Unprogrammed reinforcement of patients' behavior in a mental hospital. *Behaviour Research and Therapy,* 1967, 5, 201-207.

Goffman, E. *Asylums: Essays on the social situation of mental patients and other inmates.* Garden City, N.Y.: Anchor Books, 1961.

Graziano, A. M. Clinical innovation and the mental health power structure: A social case history. *American Psychologist,* 1969, 24, 10-18.

Greenblatt, M., Levinson, D. J. & Williams, R. H. (Eds.) *The patient and the mental hospital.* Glencoe, Ill.: Free Press, 1957.

Gurel, L. A. A forward-looking backward glance: An overview of past, present and projected program evaluation staff research. In *Highlights of the Twelfth Annual Conference in Cooperative Studies in Psychiatry.* Perry Point, Md.: Veterans Administration Central Neuropsychiatric Research Laboratory, 1967.

Hastings, D. W. Follow-up results in psychiatric illness. *American Journal of Psychiatry,* 1958, 114, 1057-1066.

Herjanic, M. & LaFave, H. G. Two years follow-up of eighty-one chronic hospitalized patients. Paper presented at a meeting of the American Psychiatric Association, Atlantic City, May 12, 1966. Cited by W. M. Mendel, On the abolition of the psychiatric hospital. In L. M. Roberts, N. S. Greenfield & M. H. Miller (Eds.), *Comprehensive mental health: The challenge of evaluation.* Madison: University of Wisconsin Press, 1968. Pp. 237-247.

Hunter, R. & Macalpine, I. (Eds.) *Three hundred years of psychiatry, 1535-1860.* London: Oxford University Press, 1963.

Johnston, R. & McNeal, B. F. Residual psychopathology in released psychiatric patients and its relation to readmission. *Journal of Abnormal Psychology,* 1965, 70, 337-342.

Jones, K. & Sidebotham, R. *Mental hospitals at work.* London: Routledge & Kegan Paul, 1962.

Klerman, G. L. The private psychiatric hospital in the community mental health era. *International Journal of Psychiatry,* 1968, 6, 437-441.

Kramer, M., Goldstein, H., Israel, R. H. & Johnson, N. A. Application of life table methodology to the study of mental hospital populations. *Psychiatric Research Techniques,* June 1956. Cited by R. B. Ellsworth, B. T. Mead & W. H. Clayton, The rehabilitation and disposition of chronically hospitalized schizophrenic patients. *Mental Hygiene,* 1958, 42, 343-348.

Kubie, L. The future of the psychiatric hospital. *International Journal of Psychiatry,* 1968, 6, 419-433. (a)

Kubie, L. Reply to Dr. Klerman. *International Journal of Psychiatry,* 1968, 6, 449-450. (b)

Lehrman, N. S. Do our hospitals help make acute schizophrenia chronic? *Diseases of the Nervous System,* 1961, 22, 489-493.

Lewinsohn, P. M. & Nichols, R. C. The evaluation of changes in psychiatric patients during and after hospitalization. *Journal of Clinical Psychology,* 1964, 20, 272-279.

Longabaugh, R., Eldred, S. H., Bell, N. W. & Sherman, L. J. The interactional world of the chronic schizophrenic patient. *Psychiatry,* 1966, 29, 78-99.

Longnecker, E., Miller, D., Richardson, B. & Willingham, D. Extramural treatment of acute mental illness. Unpublished master's thesis, University of Southern California School of Social Work, June 1966. Cited by W. M. Mendel, On the abolition of the psychiatric hospital. In L. M. Roberts, N. S. Greenfield & M. H. Miller (Eds.), *Comprehensive mental health: The challenge of evaluation.* Madison: University of Wisconsin Press, 1968. Pp. 237-247.

Lovaas, O. I., Freitag, G., Gold, V. J. & Kassorka, I. C. Experimental studies in childhood schizophrenia: Analysis of self-destructive behavior. *Journal of Experimental Child Psychology,* 1965, 2, 67-84.

Mahrer, A. R. Psychological symptoms as a function of psychiatric hospitalization. *Psychological Reports,* 1963, 13, 266.

Mahrer, A. R. & Mason, D. Changes in number of self-reported symptoms during psychiatric hospitalization. *Journal of Consulting Psychology,* 1965, 29, 285.

Masserman, J. H. & Carmichael, H. T. Diagnosis and prognosis in psychiatry: With a follow-up study of the results of short-term general hospital therapy of psychiatric cases. *Journal of Mental Science,* 1938, 84, 893-946.

McPartland, T. S. General summary. In R. L. Epps & L. D. Hanes (Eds.), *Day care of psychiatric patients.* Springfield: Charles C. Thomas, 1964. Pp. 141-151.

McPartland, R. S. & Richart, R. H. Social and clinical outcomes of psychiatric treatment. *Archives of General Psychiatry,* 1966, 14, 179-184.

Mendel, W. M. Brief hospitalization techniques. In J. H. Masserman (Ed.), *Current psychiatric therapies, 1966,* Vol. 6. New York: Grune & Stratton, 1966. Pp. 310-316. (a)

Mendel, W. M. Effect of length of hospitalization on rate and quality of remission from acute psychotic episodes. *Journal of Nervous and Mental Diseases,* 1966, 143, 226-233. (b)

Mendel, W. M. Tranquilizer prescribing as a function of the experience and availability of the therapist. *American Journal of Psychiatry,* 1967, 124, 54-60.

Mendel, W. M. On the abolition of the psychiatric hospital. In L. M. Roberts, N. S. Greenfield & M. H. Miller (Eds.), *Comprehensive mental health: The challenge of evaluation.* Madison: University of Wisconsin Press, 1968. Pp. 237-247.

Mendel, W. M. & Rapport, S. Determinants of the decision for psychiatric hospitalization. Paper presented at the annual meetings of the American Psychiatric Association, Boston, May, 1968.

Meyerson, A. Theory and principles of the "total push" method in the treatment of chronic schizophrenics. *American Journal of Psychiatry,* 1939, 95, 1197-1204.

Morrissey, J. R. *The case for family care of the mentally ill.* New York: Behavioral Publications, 1967. (Community Mental Health Journal Monograph No. 2)

Norris, V. *Mental illness in London.* London: Chapman & Hall, 1959. (Maudsley Monograph No. 6)

Perrow, C. Hospitals: Technology, structure and goals. In J. G. March (Ed.), *Handbook of organizations.* Chicago: Rand McNally, 1965. Pp. 910-971.

Pritchard, M. & Graham, P. An investigation of a group of patients who have attended both the child and adult departments of the same psychiatric hospital. *British Journal of Psychiatry,* 1966, 112, 603-612.

Rapoport, R. N., Rapoport, R. & Rosow, I. *Community as doctor: New perspectives on a therapeutic community.* London: Tavistock, 1960.

Sanders, R., Smith, R. S. & Weinmann, B. S. *Chronic psychoses and recovery.* San Francisco: Jossey-Bass, 1967.

Schwartz, M. S. What is a therapeutic milieu? In M. Greenblatt, D. J. Levinson & R. H. Williams (Eds.), *The patient and the mental hospital.* Glencoe, Ill.: Free Press, 1957. Pp. 130-144.

Schwartz, M. S. & Shockley, E. L. *The nurse and the mental patient.* New York: Russell Sage Foundation, 1956.

Silverstein, M. *Psychiatric aftercare.* Philadelphia: University of Pennsylvania Press, 1968.

Solomon, D. N. Professional persons in bureaucratic organizations. In Walter Reed Army Institute of Research, *Symposium on preventive and social psychiatry, April 15-17, 1957.* Washington, D.C.: U.S. Government Printing Office, 1957. Pp. 253-270.

Sommer, R. & Osmond, H. Symptoms of institutional care. *Social Problems,* 1961, 8, 254-263.

Stimpert, W. E., Sinnett, E. R. & Wilkins, D. M. A description of psychiatric patients five years after treatment. *Social Work,* 1966, 11, 78-86.

Strassman, H. D., Thaler, M. B. & Schein, E. H. A prisoner of war syndrome: Apathy as a reaction to severe stress. *American Journal of Psychiatry,* 1956, 112, 998-1003.

Stuart, R. B. Critical reappraisal and reformulation of selected "mental health" programs. Paper presented at First Banff International Conference on Behavior Modification, Banff, Alberta, Canada, April 3-5, 1969.

Ullmann, L. P. *Institution and outcome: A comparative study of psychiatric hospitals.* Oxford, England: Pergamon Press, 1967.

Vitale, J. Mental hospital therapy: A review and integration. In J. H. Masserman (Ed.), *Current psychiatric therapies,* Vol. 2. New York: Grune & Stratton, 1962. Pp. 247-265.

von Brauchitsch, H. Growing up in a mental hospital. Paper presented at the meeting of the Michigan Association of Neuropsychiatric Hospital and Clinic Physicians, Ypsilanti, Michigan, Fall, 1965.

von Brauchitsch, H. The "schizophrenic" hospital. Paper presented at the meeting of the World Congress of Psychiatry, Madrid, September, 1966.

3
Failure and Deterioration Associated with Psychotherapy

Psychotherapy has been variously defined in ways consonant with the theoretical persuasions of different authors. Most definitions of psychotherapy have in common the planful management of an interpersonal process in an effort to relieve the patient's initial distress and enhance his subsequent functioning. Some of these approaches rely upon cognitive change, others rely upon change mediated by direct interpersonal manipulation, and still others utilize planned therapeutic noninvolvement. Differences in theory and technique notwithstanding, J. D. Frank (1961) has observed:

> Statistical studies of psychotherapy consistently report that
> about two-thirds of neurotic patients. . .are improved immedi-
> ately after treatment, regardless of the type of psychotherapy
> they have received, and the same improvement rate has been
> found for patients who have not received any treatment that
> was deliberately psychotherapeutic [pp. 13-14].

There are several plausible explanations for this finding. First, it could be concluded that the change associated with psychotherapy may have little dependence upon the explicit theory of psychotherapy. For example, Frank (1962) has suggested that the presentation of a coherent theoretical explanation for distress may aid the patient no matter what the content of the theory may be, while Glover (1955) has suggested that patients may improve even when offered "inexact interpretations" of their psychopathology. Second, it could be concluded that virtually no aspect of the treatment process is as beneficial as the passage of time which is associated with the amelioration of situational stresses or just with maturation. This is the basis of Myerson's (1939) early disclaimer about psychotherapy. He said:

> The neuroses are 'cured' by Christian Science, osteopathy, chiropractic, nux vomica and bromides, benzedrine sulfate, change of scene, a blow on the head, and psychoanalysis, which probably means that none of these has yet established its real worth in the matter. . .Moreover, since many neuroses are self-limited, anyone who spends two years with a patient gets credit for the operation of nature [p. 641].

When this was written, Myerson was undoubtedly familiar with Curran's (1937) data showing that 61 per cent of the untreated or inadequately treated patients showed marked changes, while relatively simple techniques were shown to be effective in aiding the treated group of patients.

A third explanation for the observed comparability of the effects of heterogeneous treatments may be the operation of response bias in those who make ratings of improvement. It is generally agreed, for example, that consensually valid definitions of mental health are lacking (Scott, 1961) and that when definitions are offered they are often based "solely on the value system of the author using the term [Ginsberg, 1955, p. 6]." Also, while there may be agreement about the extreme evaluations of acceptable and unacceptable behavior, the bulk of patients in the middle group are less susceptible to precise identification because these decisions "depend upon social norms which allow for considerable variability from what is recognized as typical or expected behavior [Burdock & Hardesty, 1964, p. 59]." Lacking clearcut criteria of acceptable functioning, judgments about patient change must be based upon therapist impression—and many therapists may be presumed to be impressed by their own competence.

These problems in the definition and objectification of psychotherapy must be taken into account in evaluating the results of psychotherapy. The difficulties in making such an evaluation are compounded by the shifting nature of the field of psychotherapy, which is at once so vast and so malleable. With these qualifications in mind, the following data are offered as a partial assessment of the effects of psychotherapy.

Empirical Findings in Psychotherapy Research

Reviews of the outcome studies of psychotherapy tend to reflect the biases of their authors. For example, Cross (1964) reviewed nine studies, of which six supported the effectiveness of psychotherapy; in this chapter twenty-one studies will be cited, of which only two are positive. The differences in the conclusions are naturally a consequence both of the specific studies which are included and the manner in which their results are interpreted.

Reviewers who stress studies utilizing "pre-experimental designs" (Campbell & Stanley, 1963) are likely to show strong positive results for psychotherapy. Pre-experimental designs usually compare the behavior of one group of individuals before and after they receive psychotherapy. If changes occur, they are attributed to the intervention, although a great many other variables (such as maturation of the client, nonspecific therapeutic factors like the "personality" of the therapist, and other totally unrelated events in the patients' lives) may make as strong a contribution to the observed outcome as does the specific therapy itself.

In addition, the psychotherapy research which employs pre-experimental designs is likely to take the form of a single therapist's attempt to demonstrate the effectiveness of his own treatment based upon his own evaluation of its outcome. These results are naturally subject to intense and inherent bias, as few therapists are likely to publish reports which do not support their personal convictions.

Typical of the reports in this category is the study by Heilbrunn (1963) in which the author reviewed his treatment of 241 private patients over a 15-year period. He used his own evaluation of their improvement or nonimprovement and found that 27 per cent of the patients seen less than 20 times were rated as improved while 38 per cent of the patients seen from 301-1,350 times (average, 509) were rated as improved. In an earlier report in the same vein, Heilbrunn (1962) reported an improvement rate of 41 per cent for patients who received psychoanalytic therapy for an average of 424 hours over an average period of 3.1 years.

Heilbrunn was careful to include in his study all of the patients whom he treated. Other authors do not exercise this caution. For example, the Chicago Institute for Psycho-analysis (1937) reported an average of approximately 60 per cent effectiveness of *completed* psychoanalytic therapies. The patients who terminated treatment before completion were not included in this result, and it is estimated that their inclusion would cut the reported success rate in half (Masserman & Carmichael, 1938). The exact effect of this handling of data can be seen in Knight's (1941) study of the effects of psychoanalytic therapy. His patient sample included 952 patients. From this number, he deleted 216 patients who had "severe" problems. Of the remaining 736 patients, 205 terminated in less than six months and would have been excluded from the Chicago study. Of the remaining 531 patients, 158 were regarded as nonsignificantly improved and 54 as unchanged or worse, leaving 319 patients who were significantly improved. This group represents 60 per cent of the final 531 patients but only 34 per cent of the original 952 patients. It can therefore be seen that the research reporter has wide latitude in the manner in which he controls his data, and can materially affect the outcome of his investi-gation in this manner. Parenthetically, the criteria used for evaluation of patients included their estimated degree of symptomatology, interpersonal relations, sexual adjustment, and productivity. Each of these factors is distinctly vulner-able to biased evaluation.

In addition to including all treated cases, a second improvement in this type of pre-experimental design is the utilization of measures of outcome which are more objective than therapist opinion. As an illustration, Dymond (1955) compared the performance of six clients who successfully completed "client-centered therapy" with the performance of eight who did not complete treatment. As measures, she used both a Q-sort of self-descriptive items and the Thematic Apperception Test. She found no significant before-after differences on either measure. The clear advantage of using measures independent of therapist opinion is avoidance of the danger that the therapist will rate more highly those patients who choose to remain in contact with him for longer periods of time, independent of whether they showed improvement legitimately attributable to the effects of the treatment they received.

Besides pre-experimental designs, psychotherapy research often takes the form of quasi-experimental or experimental designs (Campbell & Stanley, 1963). These designs utilize control group comparisons in order to contrast the degree of change noted in patients who do and do not receive a particular treatment. In order for these designs to truly isolate the effects of treatment, several rigorous conditions must be met, including random assignment of patients to different treatment conditions, specification of the precise nature of the treatment offered, control for the effects of before and after measurements which may themselves promote some degree of change, and control for such extratherapeutic factors as situational changes. The care taken in observing these rigors determines whether a study is classed as quasi-experimental or truly experimental. Few studies are rigorous in this sense, but an outstanding example (drawn from behavior therapy rather than psychotherapy) is the work of Gordon Paul (1966). The relative paucity of such research is probably not so much a matter of experimenter disinterest as it is a consequence of the prohibitive costs involved in carefully executed research.

The two general subtypes of quasi-experimental and experimental designs contrast the effects of more or less intense applications of the same treatment or the effects of differing treatments. A good example of the first group is found in the social work literature dealing with multiproblem families in a public assistance setting. Wallace and Smith (1968) studied the effects of intensive and routine service offered to clients receiving public assistance and found that:

> After two years of service to multi-problem families by trained caseworkers, operating with reduced caseloads and with special cooperation of the community's resources, but within the framework of public assistance policies and procedures, the demonstration group showed a small but statistically non-significant margin of improvement over the control group(s) which received only routine service from regular public assistance workers [p. 151].

A good example of research contrasting the effects of different treatment modalities within the same general framework is the work of Meyer, Borgatta and Jones (1965). They studied a large population of 381 girls in a vocational high school who were offered social casework, social group work or no treatment. They found no significant differences in such objective criteria as completion of school, grades, unexcused absences, deportment ratings and responses to standardized test batteries. In a similar vein, Ashby, Ford, Guerney and Guerney (1957) compared the effects of "non-directive" and "interpretive" treatments averaging 13 sessions and found no significant differences in any of the measures of outcome; Barendregt (1961) compared the effects of psycho-analysis (47 patients), psychotherapy (79 patients) and no-treatment controls (74 patients), and found a significant difference in only one (Neuroticism Scale) of seven indices including the Thematic Apperception Test and Rorschach test; and Barron and Leary (1955) compared the effects of individual, group or no treatment offered to 150 psychoneurotics who improved independent of the type of treatment offered.

In general, it can be said that in contrast to pre-experimental studies which typically report between 24 (Strauss, 1947) and 54 (Harrower, 1965) per cent improvement, the quasi-experimental and experimental studies do not show that treated patients outperform their untreated or differentially treated counterparts (Adamson & Dunham, 1956; Bergin, 1966; Schofield, 1964). When differences do appear between experimentals and controls, they are typically modest (Bergin, 1966; Volsky, Magoon, Norman & Hoyt, 1965) or they are found to disappear at times of follow-up (Koegler & Brill, 1967; Stone, Frank, Nash & Imber, 1961).

On the other hand, some studies reveal that controls outperform their treated counterparts (Eysenck, 1965), and other studies show that while some subjects improve following treatment, other treated subjects deteriorate as a consequence of treatment. Butler (1960), Bergin (1963, 1966) and D. S. Cartwright (1956) have cited this deterioration with the general population of psychotherapy patients. Wertham (1950) has cited illustrations in support of his view that as many as 60 per cent of psychoanalyses are harmful. Studies reviewed by Levitt (1957) show a highly variable effect of treatment, ranging from essentially positive (Irgens, 1963) to essentially negative (Maas, Kahn, Stein & Summer, 1955).

When the patients are offenders, and when performance data consists of objective measures of their rate of crime, the results are more clear-cut. For example, the early conclusion of the Cambridge-Somerville juvenile delinquency project (that "none of the evaluative methods employed indicates any degree of success for the treatment program [Powers & Witmer, 1951, p. xix; see also W. McCord & J. McCord, 1959]") has been amended to suggest that boys who received psychotherapy were more likely to be convicted of subsequent offenses (Teuber & Powers, 1953). In a similar vein, Lohman and his associates (1967) reported that 37.5 per cent of the adult offenders who had received maximum supervision including psychotherapy had parole violations, while violations were recorded for only 22.2 per cent of the offenders receiving minimal supervision. In view of this evidence, it can be said that persons who enter psychotherapy do so with a modest chance of marked improvement, a much greater chance of experiencing little or no change, and a modest chance of experiencing a deterioration in their functioning. In the words of Truax and Carkhuff (1967), "Psychotherapy may be harmful as often as helpful, with an average effect comparable to receiving no help [p. 21]."

There are several commonly noted explanations for the mischances in psychotherapy. Some researchers have sought to explain the failure and deterioration associated with psychotherapy as a consequence of client characteristics (Kirtner & D. S. Cartwright, 1958a, 1958b), although it would seem illogical to hold the patient responsible for failure in treatment which is presumably oriented to overcoming his problems. Additional explanations of failure can be attributed to therapist characteristics and treatment techniques. Characteristics such as the amount of experience of the therapist (R. D. Cartwright & Vogel, 1960; Gonyea, 1963), amount of confidence that the therapist has in himself (Kemp & Carson, 1967) and degree of therapist-patient similarity (McNair, Lorr & Callahan, 1962) have all been correlated with the degree of change.

At least three groups of techniques have also been related to treatment failures. First, the failure of therapists to display a necessary level of empathy and understanding has been correlated with deterioration (Truax, 1963). Second, it has been shown that therapist reinforcement of patient pathology may lead to deterioration (Betz, 1962; Dinoff, Rickard, Salzberg & Sipprelle, 1960; Searles, 1958). Third, therapist specificity and directiveness have been associated with positive outcomes (Gordon, 1957; Kanfer & Marston, 1964; Ryan, 1967; Speisman, Lazarus, Mordkoff & Davidson, 1964), and it may be presumed that their absence is associated with the failure of treatment under certain circumstances.

Limitations of Psychoanalysis

Most of the currently accepted approaches to psychotherapy owe their roots, if not their present structure, to psychoanalytic theory. In pursuing answers to the dilemmas posed by research dealing with the outcome of treatment, one is compelled to carefully review psychoanalytic theory and its assumptions. First, the theory has been shown to be unscientific because the terms of the theory are not objectively verifiable. Nagel (1959) has indicated that the terms of a scientific theory must meet two criteria. First:

> It must be possible to deduce determinate consequences from the assumptions of theory, so that one can decide on the basis of logical considerations, and prior to the examination of any empirical data, whether or not an alleged consequence of the theory is indeed implied by the latter [pp. 39-40].

Lorand (1946) has provided a telling illustration of the effects of violations of this requirement. He describes a patient having a dream about a man who is crossing a street while smiling and wearing a hat. He offers interpretations of the dream as clear-cut indicators of masculinity and of femininity and observes: "Although these two interpretations differ widely, both have validity and may describe the content of the patient's unconscious [Lorand, 1946, pp. 190-191]." Freud (1949) also illustrates this sophistry, as in the following comment:

> The symptoms of neurosis are exclusively, it might be said, either a substitutive satisfaction of some sexual impulse or measures to prevent such a satisfaction, and are as a rule compromises between the two [p. 85].

Because exactly contradictory inferences can be drawn from the same observations, it is impossible to make univalent hypotheses and therefore it is impossible to reject the assumptions of psychoanalytic theory. Based upon such an insubstantial theory, it is equally hazardous to contemplate therapeutic maneuvers.

The second requirement for scientific theory laid down by Nagel (1959) is:

> At least some theoretical notions must be tied down to fairly definite and unambiguously specified observable materials by ways of rules of procedure variously called 'correspondence rules,' 'coordinating definitions,' and 'operational definitions' [p. 40].

The absence of operational definitions for such essential terms as "ego," "impulse" and "cathexis" has led to a circularity based upon the interrelationship of terms which are wholly definitional in character. The effect of this circularity is illustrated by Snygg and Combs (1950), who cite the following exchange:

> 'Why did you do that, Frances?' she was asked.
> 'Oh, my brain told me to do it.'
> 'Well, why did your brain tell you to do it?'
> 'Oh (with a giggle), I guess its brain told it to do it' [p. 526].

One can easily substitute the term "ego" for brain and clearly demonstrate the circularity of psychoanalytic reasoning, as it can be shown that second-order concepts are used to explain first-order concepts which are, in turn, unverified inferences from behavioral observations.

It may be unjust to attack the inherent logic of the psychoanalytic approach because Freud himself referred to psychoanalytic theory as "metapsychological [Freud, 1956c, p. 114]." Nevertheless, as long as psychoanalysis fails to define its basic elements operationally, it is not possible to evaluate its effectiveness objectively (Leo, 1968, p. 58), because every term is applicable to every patient (Schafer, 1950). Furthermore, it may not even be possible to determine when psychoanalysis has taken place because "the attempt to define psychoanalysis itself results in controversy [Davidman, 1964, p. 34]."

A second limitation in the psychoanalytic approach stems from the invalidity of some of its basic assumptions. Despite the fact that Freud recognized that a knowledge of early traumatic situations may not necessarily lead to alleviation of the patient's problems (1956a, p. 362), he generally asserted:

> . . .the actual conflict of the neurotic becomes comprehensible and capable of solution only if it can be traced back to the patient's past history, and by following the path which his libido took when his neurosis started [1938, p. 975].

Unfortunately, however, some of the basic assumptions which Freud made concerning the connection between early life experience and adult behavior have not been validated by subsequent, careful research (Caldwell, 1964; Hovey, 1959; Sewell, 1952). For example, Sears (1943) reviewed 166 studies purportedly linking childhood experience with adult behavior and concluded that "perhaps a dozen other theories would provide as good or better explanations of the facts [p. 134]," while Orlansky (1949) reviewed data pertaining to the effects of breast feeding, sphincter training, frustration and restriction of movement upon adult behavior, and concluded that ". . .personality is not the resultant of instinctual infantile libidinal drives mechanically channelled by parental disciplines, but rather that it is a dynamic product of the interaction of a unique organism undergoing maturation and a unique physical and social environment [p. 39]." This nonspecific association of the general characteristics of the infant's early life environment and his adult personality has been well-substantiated (Becker, 1964; Chess, Thomas & Birch, 1959; McCord & McCord, 1958; Yarrow, 1964), but these conclusions are at best scantily related to the Freudian assumptions. Studies of correlation between the child's behavior and his responses as an adult have shown that many of the observed relationships are irrelevant to Freudian assumptions (Hearn, Charles & Wolins, 1965), while others simply do not offer substantiating evidence. As an illustration of the latter research, Livson and Peskin (1967) have shown that the behavior of "oedipal," "latency" and adolescent children do not correlate with adult behavior, but children's behavior at puberty does serve as a predictor of their adult behavior.

While the hypothetical relationship between specific child-rearing practices and adult behavior has not been substantiated, hypotheses concerning the immediate effects of selected practices, such as modeling (Bandura & Walters, 1963) and positive reinforcement of problematic behaviors (Ferster, 1961; Williams, 1959), have received strong support. Also, interesting hypotheses concerning the relationship between communicational mode and behavioral disturbance have been set forth and partially validated (Bateson, Jackson, Haley & Weakland, 1959; Watzlawick, 1963), although not completely so (Ringuette & Kennedy, 1966). In general, however, it has not been demonstrated that any specific set of family interaction patterns has a necessary outcome as measured by any specific response pattern (G. H. Frank, 1965). Perhaps the most convincing evidence of all, however, has demonstrated an association between factors of social class and the development of certain types of behavioral disturbance (Dohrenwend & Dohrenwend, 1965; Hardt & Feinhandler, 1959), as well as the ascription of diagnostic labels (Hollingshead & Redlich, 1958). Thus theories which materially differ from Freud's view are supported while his notions still await confirmation.

A third major area of weakness in the psychoanalytic approach is found in the Freudian recommendations pertaining to the behavior of the therapist. Freud (1956b) suggests, for example, that the therapist should "be impenetrable to the patient, and, like a mirror, reflect nothing but what is shown to him [p. 331]." Furthermore, it is recommended that he "take as a model in psycho-analytic treatment the surgeon who puts aside all his own feelings, including that of human sympathy, and concentrates his mind on one single purpose, that of performing the operation as skillfully as possible [Freud, 1956b, p. 327]." Contrary to his own strictures, however, Freud stated:

(1) "We serve the patient in various functions as an authority and a substitute for his parents, as a teacher and educator. . .[1949, p. 77]."

(2)   "...we have to admit that we have only abandoned hypnosis in our methods in order to discover suggestion again in the shape of transference [1935, pp. 387-388]."

(3)   "...the personal influence of the analyst...does exist, and plays a big part in the analysis [1950, p. 25]."

(4)   "This personal influence is our strongest dynamic weapon, it is this new factor which we bring to the situation, to make it fluid. The intellectual validity of our explanations cannot achieve that, since the patient shares all the prejudices current in our surrounding world, and may as little believe us as do our scientific critics. The neurotic sets himself to the work because he believes in the analyst, and he believes in him because he begins to entertain certain feelings towards him [1950, p. 82]."

The therapist who would read and seek to apply Freudian recommendations is therefore confronted with strictly paradoxical sets of commands—on the one hand appearing neutral to his patient while on the other serving as a guiding force—with no reasonable way to clarify the inconsistencies, if indeed it were possible to refrain from influencing the patient (Salter, 1949).

The problem of therapist influence is pointedly cited by Freud, who nevertheless appears to reject its importance. Freud (1956b) acknowledged that both dreams and their latent content are susceptible "to influence from 'suggestion' by the physician [p. 141]," but continued to regard dreams as "the most favorable object of our study [1949, p. 47]." The direct influence of the analyst upon the dreams of his patient is shown by Salter (1949, p. 91), who refers to Freudian, Jungian and Adlerian patients having Freudian, Jungian and Adlerian dreams respectively. In another place, Salter (1963) characterizes this problem in even more specific terms:

Analytic therapy, I think, is actually more like 'salting' a mine. The analyst sprinkles and buries false nuggets of Oedipus, castration (or penis envy), and bisexuality. Then as the patient digs (where he is directed to dig) and discovers the planted material, the analyst is convinced that he has struck pay dirt.

> I think that any archaeologist who, under cover of darkness, buried spurious relics in order to unearth them the next day, would hardly be considered honorable. Yet the analysts do precisely this, quite sincerely and in open daylight. For it is by *suggestion* that the analysts implant their preposterous 'discoveries' in the minds of their patients, and it is by *suggestion* that the patient is taught to find what he never possessed in the first place [p. 46].

Apart from introducing what may be a profoundly irrelevant body of material into the patient's treatment, the introduction of such dream sequences has, in Salter's (1963, p. 86) estimation, the additional disadvantage of encouraging the patient to ignore the pressing problems of his current reality in an effort to pursue the elusive figures of his dreams.

A fourth limitation in the psychoanalytic approach has to do with the general relationship between the therapist and his patient. Freud called for the maximal use of transference ("...a form of resistance. The patient defends himself against remembering and discussing his infantile conflicts by reliving them....a general human trait to interpret one's experiences in the light of the past [Fenichel, 1945, pp. 29-30]"). Freud (1950) said of the transference:

> ... like every love affair, it pushes all other mental activities out of the way; it wipes out interest in the treatment and in improvement, and in short, we can be in no doubt that it has usurped the place of the neurosis, and our work has had the result of replacing one form of illness by another [p. 84].

There is therefore a calculated risk involved at the basis of psychoanalytic treatment in which the patient is encouraged to develop a transitory form of neurosis which may, upon being unleashed, become unmasterable so that the "analysis must be broken off [Freud, 1950, p. 87]." Thus, being cognizant of the risks inherent in his treatment approach, Freud (1950) speculated that there are times when "you cannot count at all on [the patient's] cooperation and compliance [because] he does not want to become well at all... His Ego has lost its unity, so it has no single-minded purpose.

If he were otherwise, he would not be a neurotic [pp. 76-77]." Finally, if the patient succeeds in mastering the transference and the rationalizations of his therapist, Freud (1953a) identified a rather limited goal occasioned by the completion of psychoanalysis when he stated:

> Our impression is that we must not be surprised if the differ-
> ence between a person who has not and a person who has
> been analysed is, after all, not so radical as we endeavour to
> make it and expect and assert that it will be [p. 329].

The final criticism of the psychoanalytic approach to be cited here is its self-imposed insensitivity to criticism. For example, when Freud's theory of sexuality was criticized on empirical grounds (as it was by Sears in 1944), Freud's (1950) response took the following form:

> I know, of course, that the recognition we afford to sexuality
> is—whether they confess it or not—the strongest motive for
> our opponents' hostility to psychoanalysis. But are we to let
> ourselves be shaken on that account? It only shows us how
> neurotic our whole cultural life is, when people apparently
> normal behave no differently from neurotics [p. 54].

Thus the typical Freudian response to criticism was to accuse the critic of neuroticism rather than to adduce data in defense of the position that was under attack. Following from this position, Freudians tend to accuse their detractors and those who criticize the sexuality doctrine of incomplete understanding because they have not undergone the process of self-disclosure in psychoanalytic treatment. For example, Freud (1949) has said:

> The teachings of psychoanalysis are based upon an incalculable
> number of observations and experiences, and no one who has
> not repeated those observations upon himself or upon others
> is in a position to arrive at an independent judgment of it
> [p. 9].

To this Jastrow (1932) has responded:

> Even if I had the proverbial nine lives to live, I should not feel
> the obligation to devote one apiece to the practice of physiog-

nomy, phrenology, astrology, numerology. . .and Freudian psychoanalysis, in order. . .to indicate the gross and flagrant violations of logic and sanity which they present [pp. 265-266].

Summary

In summary, it can be said that the patient who enters psychotherapy does so not without a distinct risk of deterioration or of simply wasting his time and money. The explanation of this fact pursued in this chapter has been the weakness in the psychoanalytic approach that has spawned most of the current psychotherapeutic approaches. One of the weaknesses is the limitation of psychodynamic theory (Skinner, 1954) which does not permit adequate testing of postdictive inferences. A second limitation is the invulnerability of the theory and its adherents to adverse data. The general limitations of the treatment approach have been widely acknowledged for some time (Colby, 1964).

The adverse evidence is particularly compelling because the treatments have been carried out with patients drawn from the "more favored" groups of the society, who are presumably most free of situational stress (Cowen & Zax, 1967, p. 17). Despite this state of affairs, psychoanalytic treatment procedures basically have not been subjected to a self-corrective process, and one astute critic, Dr. F. C. Redlich, Dean of the School of Medicine at Yale University, has observed: "Almost everything we know about psychoanalysis today was Freud's single-handed and single-minded work [cited by Leo, 1968, p. 58]," while the psychoanalytic world remains "a rigidly dogmatic and defensive guild, not plugged into the major intellectual currents of the day [Leo, 1968, p. 58]."

These critical comments are far less applicable to other psychotherapeutic approaches which are the product of more careful research—e. g., client centered therapy—but even these treatments have shown themselves to be vulnerable to harmful or "psychonoxious" (Truax and Carkhuff, 1967, p. 20) effects.

References

Adamson, L. & Dunham, H. W. Clinical treatment of male delinquents: A case study in effort and result. *American Sociological Review,* 1956, 21, 312-320.

Ashby, J. D., Ford, D. H., Guerney, B. G. & Guerney, L. F. Effects on clients of a reflective and leading type of psychotherapy. *Psychological Monographs,* 1957, 71 (24, Whole No. 453).

Bandura, A. & Walters, R. H. *Social learning and personality development.* New York: Holt, Rinehart & Winston, 1963.

Barendregt, J. T. *Psychological Studies,* Vol. 1. *Research in psychodiagnostics.* The Hague, Netherlands: Mouton, 1961.

Barron, F. & Leary, T. F. Changes in psychoneurotic patients with and without psychotherapy. *Journal of Consulting Psychology,* 1955, 19, 239-245.

Bateson, G., Jackson, D., Haley, J. & Weakland, H. The genesis of mental disorders and social deviance. *Behavioral Science,* 1956, 1, 251-264.

Becker, W. Consequences of different kinds of parental discipline. In M. L. Hoffman & L. W. Hoffman (Eds.), *Review of child development research,* Vol. 1. New York: Russell Sage Foundation, 1964. Pp. 169-208.

Bergin, A. E. The effects of psychotherapy: Negative results revisited. *Journal of Counseling Psychology,* 1963, 10, 244-250.

Bergin, A. E. Some implications of psychotherapy research for therapeutic practice. *Journal of Abnormal Psychology,* 1966, 71, 235-246.

Betz, B. J. Experiences in research on psychotherapy with schizophrenic patients. In H. H. Strupp & L. Luborsky (Eds.), *Research in psychotherapy.* Washington, D.C.: American Psychological Association, 1962. Pp. 41-60.

Burdock, E. I. & Hardesty, A. S. Quantitative techniques for the evaluation of psychiatric treatment. In P. H. Hoch & J. Zubin (Eds.), *The evaluation of psychiatric treatment.* New York: Grune & Stratton, 1964. Pp. 58-74.

Butler, J. M. Self-concept change in psychotherapy. *Counseling Center Discussion Papers,* University of Chicago, 1960, 6:13, 1-27.

Caldwell, B. M. The effects of infant care. In M. L. Hoffman & L. W. Hoffman (Eds.), *Review of child development research,* Vol. 1. New York: Russell Sage Foundation, 1964. Pp. 9-87.

Campbell, D. T. & Stanley, J. C. *Experimental and quasi-experimental designs for research.* Chicago: Rand McNally, 1963.

Cartwright, D. S. Note on changes in psychoneurotic patients with and without psychotherapy. *Journal of Consulting Psychology,* 1956, 20, 403-404.

Cartwright, R. D. & Vogel, J. L. A comparison of changes in psychoneurotic patients during matched periods of therapy and no therapy. *Journal of Consulting Psychology,* 1960, 24, 121-127.

Chess, S., Thomas, A. & Birch, H. Characteristics of the individual child's behavioral responses to the environment. *American Journal of Orthopsychiatry,* 1959, 29, 791-802.

Chicago Institute for Psycho-analysis. Five year report (1932-1937). Mimeo, 1937.

Colby, K. M. Psychotherapeutic processes. In P. R. Farnsworth & Q. McNemar (Eds.), *Annual Review of Psychology*, Vol. 15. Palo Alto, Calif.: Annual Reviews, 1964. Pp. 347-370.

Cowen, E. L. & Zax, M. The mental health fields today: Issues and problems. In E. L. Cowen, E. A. Gardner & M. Zax (Eds.), *Emergent approaches to mental health problems.* New York: Appleton-Century-Crofts, 1967. Pp. 3-29.

Cross, H. J. The outcome of psychotherapy: A selected analysis of research findings. *Journal of Consulting Psychology,* 1964, 25, 413-418.

Curran, D. The problem of assessing psychiatric treatment: St. George's Hospital. *The Lancet,* 1937, 233, 1005.

Davidman, H. Evaluation of psychoanalysis: A clinician's view. In P. H. Hoch & J. Zubin (Eds.), *The evaluation of psychiatric treatment.* New York: Grune & Stratton, 1964. Pp. 32-44.

Dinoff, M., Rickard, H. C., Salzberg, H. & Sipprelle, C. N. An experimental analogue of three psychotherapeutic approaches. *Journal of Clinical Psychology,* 1960, 16, 70-73.

Dohrenwend, B. P. & Dohrenwend, B. S. The problem of validity in field studies of psychological disorder. *Journal of Abnormal Psychology,* 1965, 70, 52-69.

Dymond, R. F. Adjustment changes in the absence of psychotherapy. *Journal of Consulting Psychology,* 1955, 19, 103-107.

Eysenck, H. J. The effects of psychotherapy. *International Journal of Psychiatry,* 1965, 1, 97-144.

Fenichel, O. *The psychoanalytic theory of neurosis.* New York: Norton, 1945.

Ferster, C. B. Positive reinforcement and behavioral deficits of autistic children. *Child Development,* 1961, 32, 437-456.

Frank, G. H. The role of the family in the development of psychopathology. *Psychological Bulletin,* 1965, 64, 191-205.

Frank, J. D. *Persuasion and healing.* Baltimore: Johns Hopkins Press, 1961.

Frank, J. D. The role of cognitions in illness and healing. In H. S. Strupp & L. Luborsky (Eds.), *Research in psychotherapy.* Washington, D.C.: American Psychological Association, 1962. Pp. 1-12.

Freud, S. *General intoduction to psycho-analysis.* New York: Liveright, 1935.

Freud, S. The history of the psychoanalytic movement. In A. A. Brill (Trans. & Ed.), *The basic writings of Sigmund Freud.* New York: Random House Modern Library, 1938. Pp. 931-977.

Freud, S. *An outline of psychoanalysis.* New York: Norton, 1949.

Freud, S. *The question of lay analysis.* New York: Norton, 1950.

Freud, S. Analysis terminable and interminable. In *Collected papers,* Vol. 5. London: Hogarth Press, 1953. Pp. 316-357. (a)

Freud, S. Remarks upon the theory and practice of dream interpretation. In *Collected papers,* Vol. 5. London: Hogarth Press, 1953. Pp. 136-149. (b)

Freud, S. Further recommendations in the technique of psychoanalysis. In *Collected papers,* Vol. 2. London: Hogarth Press, 1956. Pp. 342-365. (a)

Freud, S. Recommendations for physicians on the psycho-analytic method of treatment. In *Collected papers,* Vol. 2. London: Hogarth Press, 1956. Pp. 323-333. (b)

Freud, S. The unconscious. In *Collected papers,* Vol. 4. London: Hogarth Press, 1956. Pp. 98-136. (c)

Ginsberg, S. W. The mental health movement and its theoretical assumptions. In R. Kotinsky & H. L. Witmer (Eds.), *Community programs for mental health: Theory, practice, evaluation.* Cambridge, Mass.: Harvard University Press, 1955. Pp. 1-29.

Glover, E. *The technique of psychoanalysis.* New York: International Universities Press, 1955.

Gonyea, G. C. The "ideal therapeutic relationship" and counseling outcome. *Journal of Clinical Psychology,* 1963, 19, 481-487.

Gordon, J. E. Leading and following psychotherapeutic techniques with hypnotically induced repression and hostility. *Journal of Abnormal and Social Psychology,* 1957, 54, 405-410.

Hardt, R. H. & Feinhandler, S. J. Social class and mental hospitalization prognosis. *American Sociological Review,* 1959, 24, 815-821.

Harrower, M. *Psychodiagnostic testing: An empirical approach based on a follow-up of 2,000 cases.* Springfield, Ill.: Charles C. Thomas, 1965.

Hearn, J. L., Charles, D. C. & Wolins, L. Life history antecedents of measured personality variables. *Journal of Genetic Psychology,* 1965, 107, 99-110.

Heilbrunn, G. Advances in psychoanalytic therapy. In J. H. Masserman (Ed.), *Current psychiatric therapies,* Vol. 2. New York: Grune & Stratton, 1962. Pp. 19-29.

Heilbrunn, G. Results with psychoanalytic therapy. *American Journal of Psychotherapy,* 1963, 17, 427-435.

Hollingshead, A. B. & Redlich, F. C. *Social class and mental illness.* New York: Wiley, 1958.

Hovey, H. B. The questionable validity of some assumed antecedents of mental illness. *Journal of Clinical Psychology,* 1959, 15, 270-272.

Irgens, E. M. Must parents' attitudes become modified in order to bring about adjustment in problem children? *Smith College Studies in Social Work,* 1936, 7, 17-45.

Jastrow, J. *Freud, his dream and sex theories.* Cleveland: World Publishing, 1932.

Kanfer, F. H. & Marston, A. R. Characteristics of interactional behavior in a psychotherapy analogue. *Journal of Consulting Psychology,* 1964, 28, 456-467.

Kemp, D. E. & Carson, R. C. AB therapist-type distinction, evaluation of patient characteristics, and professional training. In American Psychological Association, *Proceedings of the 75th annual convention of the APA,* Vol. 2. Washington, D.C.: American Psychological Association, 1967. Pp. 247-249.

Kirtner, W. L. & Cartwright, D. S. Success and failure in client-centered therapy as a function of client personality variables. *Journal of Consulting Psychology,* 1958, 22, 259-265. (a)

Kirtner, W. L. & Cartwright, D. S. Success and failure in client-centered therapy as a function of initial in-therapy behavior. *Journal of Consulting Psychology,* 1958, 22, 329-334. (b)

Knight, R. P. Evaluation of the results of psychoanalytic therapy. *American Journal of Psychiatry,* 1941, 98, 434-446.

Koegler, R. & Brill, N. Q. *Treatment of psychiatric outpatients.* New York: Appleton-Century-Crofts, 1967.

Leo, J. Psychoanalysis reaches a crossroad. *New York Times,* April 4, 1968, sec. 1, pp. 1, 58.

Levitt, B. E. The results of psychotherapy with children: An evaluation. *Journal of Consulting Psychology,* 1957, 21, 189-196.

Livson, N. & Peskin, H. Prediction of adult psychological health in a longitudinal study. *Journal of Abnormal Psychology,* 1967, 72, 509-518.

Lohman, J. D., Wahl, A., Carter, R. M. & Lewis, S. P. *Research report number eleven: The intensive supervision caseload: A preliminary revision.* Berkeley: University of California School of Criminology, 1967.

Lorand, S. *Technique of psychoanalytic therapy.* New York: International Universities Press, 1946.

Maas, H. S., Kahn, A. J., Stein, H. D. & Summer, D. Socio-cultural factors in psychiatric clinic services for children. *Smith College Studies in Social Work,* 1955, 25, 1-90.

Masserman, J. H. & Carmichael, H. T. Diagnosis and prognosis in psychiatry. *Journal of Mental Science,* 1938, 84, 893-946.

McCord, J. & McCord, W. The effects of parental role model on criminality. *Journal of Social Issues,* 1958, 14, 66-75.

McCord, W. & McCord, J. *Origins of crime: New evaluation of the Cambridge-Somerville youth study.* New York: Columbia University Press, 1959.

McNair, D. M., Lorr, M. & Callahan, D. M. Therapist "type" and patient response to psychotherapy. *Journal of Consulting Psychology,* 1962, 26, 425-430.

Meyer, H. J., Borgatta, E. F. & Jones, W. C. *Girls at vocational high: An experiment in social work intervention.* New York: Russell Sage Foundation, 1965.

Myerson, A. The attitude of neurologists, psychiatrists and psychologists towards psychoanalysis. *American Journal of Psychiatry,* 1939, 96, 623-641.

Nagel, E. Methodological issues in psychoanalytic theory. In S. Hook (Ed.), *Psychoanalysis: Scientific method and philosophy.* New York: Grove Press, 1959. Pp. 38-56.

Orlansky, H. Infant care and personality. *Psychological Bulletin,* 1949, 46, 1-49.

Paul, G. L. *Insight vs. desensitization in psychotherapy.* Stanford, Calif.: Stanford University Press, 1966.

Powers, E. & Witmer, H. *An experiment in the prevention of delinquency: The Cambridge-Somerville youth study.* New York: Columbia University Press, 1951.

Ringuette, E. L. & Kennedy, R. An experimental study of the double bind hypothesis. *Journal of Abnormal Psychology,* 1966, 71, 136-141.

Ryan, T. A. Effectiveness of counseling in college residence halls on students' study behavior. Mimeo progress report, Oregon State University, May, 1967.

Salter, A. *Conditioned reflex therapy.* New York: Farrar, Straus & Young, 1949.

Salter, A. *The case against psychoanalysis.* New York: Citadel Press, 1963.

Schafer, R. Review of S. Deri, *Introduction to the Szondi Test: Theory and practice. Journal of Abnormal and Social Psychology,* 1950, 45, 184-188.

Schofield, W. *Psychotherapy: The purchase of friendship.* Englewood Cliffs, N.J.: Prentice-Hall, 1964.

Scott, W. A. Research definitions of mental health and illness. In T. R. Sarbin (Ed.), *Studies in behavior pathology.* New York: Holt, Rinehart & Winston, 1961. Pp. 8-22.

Searles, H. F. The schizophrenic's vulnerability to the therapist's unconscious processes. *Journal of Nervous and Mental Diseases,* 1958, 127, 247-262.

Sears, R. R. *Survey of objective studies of psychoanalytic concepts.* New York: Social Science Research Council, 1943. (Bulletin 51)

Sears, R. R. Experimental analysis of psychoanalytic phenomenon. In J. M. Hunt (Ed.), *Personality and the behavior disorders.* New York: Roland Press, 1944. Pp. 306-332.

Sewell, W. H. Infant training and the personality of the child. *American Journal of Sociology,* 1952, 58, 150-159.

Skinner, B. F. Critique of psychoanalytic concepts and theories. *Scientific Monthly,* 1954, 79, 300-305.

Snygg, D. & Combs, A. W. The phenomenological approach and the problem of "unconscious" behavior: A reply to Dr. Smith. *Journal of Abnormal and Social Psychology,* 1950, 45, 523-528.

Speisman, J. C., Lazarus, R. S., Mordkoff, A. & Davidson, L. Experimental reduction of stress based on ego-defense theory. *Journal of Abnormal and Social Psychology,* 1964, 68, 367-380.

Stone, A. R., Frank, J. D., Nash, E. H. & Imber, S. D. An intensive five-year follow-up study of treated psychiatric outpatients. *Journal of Nervous and Mental Diseases,* 1961, 133, 410-422.

Strauss, E. B. Quo vadimis. *British Journal of Medical Psychology,* 1947, 21, 1-11.

Teuber, H. L. & Powers, E. Evaluating therapy in a delinquency prevention program. *Psychiatric Treatment,* 1953, 21, 138-147.

Truax, C. B. Effective ingredients in psychotherapy. *Journal of Counseling Psychology,* 1963, 10, 256-263.

Truax, C. B. & Carkhuff, R. R., *Toward Effective Counseling and Psychotherapy.* Chicago, Ill.: Aldine Publishing Co., 1967.

Volsky, T., Jr., Magoon, T. M., Norman, W. T. & Hoyt, D. P. *The outcomes of counseling and psychotherapy.* Minneapolis: University of Minnesota Press, 1965.

Wallace, D. & Smith, J. The study: Methodology and findings. In G. E. Brown (Ed.), *The multi-problem dilemma.* Metuchen, N.J.: Scarecrow Press, 1968. Pp. 107-161.

Watzlawick, P. A review of the double bind theory. *Family Process,* 1963, 2, 132-153.

Wertham, F. What to do till the doctor goes. *The Nation,* September 2, 1950, 205-207.

Williams, C. D. The elimination of tantrum behavior by extinction. *Journal of Abnormal and Social Psychology,* 1959, 59, 269.

Yarrow, L. J. Separation from parents during early childhood. In M. L. Hoffman & L. W. Hoffman (Eds.), *Review of child development research,* Vol. 1. New York: Russell Sage Foundation, 1964. Pp. 89-136.

4
Rx for Failure: Dispositional Diagnosis

When treatment fails, the explanation may lie with the accuracy of the diagnosis or the adequacy of the techniques used following diagnosis. In this chapter it will be argued that the structure and process of diagnosis as it is commonly undertaken in mental hygiene clinics may preclude or at least seriously reduce the probability that treatment will be effective. It will be argued that both mental status examinations and projective testing are unreliable procedures whose validity is in serious doubt, and therefore the therapist who seeks to base treatment on the results of such diagnoses is forced to premise his intervention upon a very insubstantial foundation.

The Language Systems of Assessment

There are two broad language classes available to psychologists for the description of human behavior. "Phenotypic" language is essentially concerned with a description of the surface dimensions of behavior. It is consistent with this approach, for example, to point out that a child willingly eats foods chosen from a very restricted menu or that he reads at a level well below age norm. "Genotypic" language, on the other hand, is essentially concerned with explanations of behavior in terms of subsurface dynamics. It is consistent with this approach to say that a boy who rejects many foods and reads poorly suffers from an "oral aggressive character disorder."

These two language systems are not totally independent but can be identified as opposite poles on at least two of the continua cited by R. I. Watson (1967):

(a) *Methodological objectivism–methodological subjectivism* (use of methods open to verification by another competent observer–not so open).

(b) *Quantitativism–Qualitativism* (stress upon knowledge which is countable or measurable–upon that which is different in kind or essence) [p. 437].

An additional way of distinguishing the two language systems is the stress of the phenotypic system upon what a person does, in contrast to the stress of the genotypic system upon what a person presumably is. Adherents of the former approach claim that their emphasis upon observable actions validates their claim to having a system of higher scientific calibre, while adherents of the latter approach claim that their emphasis upon general predispositional characteristics validates their claim to having a system with greater explanatory power.

One of the foremost accomplishments of the phenotypic group has been Ogden Lindsley's (1956, 1960, 1963) demonstration that psychotics can be differentiated from non-psychotics through measurement of free-operant response rates. Among the more important implications of Lindsley's work is its demonstration that patients can be reliably divided into two groups solely on the basis of objectively measured behavior, and that in order to validly assign patients to different groups it is essential to count the relative frequencies of specific responses and to describe the context in which these responses are emitted. (Similar work has been done with autistic children–Ferster, 1961–and with retardates–Barrett & Lindsley, 1962.)

Genotypic diagnosis, on the other hand, relies essentially upon a Kraepelinean model which postulates qualitative differences between groups of patients. These groupings are based upon an assumption that patients who manifest certain signs can be assumed to have generalized behavioral response dispositions related to such signs. At the highest level, these dispositional assessments are probabilistic in nature. For example, Meehl (1960) has defined them in the following terms:

> Having observed one or more episodes of a given kind, we make an inductive inference as to the strength of low order *dispositions* which these episodes exemplify. Such dispositions are grouped into families, the justification for this grouping being. . .some kind of covariation. . .among the members of the dispositional family. It is perhaps possible to formulate the the clinician's decision making behavior entirely in terms of such disposition-classes. In such a formulation, clinical inference involves probabilistic transition from episodes to dispositions, followed by the attribution of further dispositions as yet unobserved [p. 20].

It is important to note that dispositions are derived by inference from observational data and they are not isomorphic with this data. That is, dispositions are logical rather than empirical entities. To say that a man has "paranoid tendencies" is to say that he has been observed to be suspicious and to *infer* that he will also be fearful and envious. Dispositional diagnosis draws upon both "signs" which are objective indicators of abnormality and "symptoms" which are indirect descriptions of subjectively perceived abnormality (Holmes, 1946) in classifying patients according to present and potential states and behavior.

Both language classes are available to the psychodiagnostician. A selection of which terms to employ should be based upon the measurable performance of each in the five major functions of diagnosis:

(1)　To describe the presenting problem

(2)　To identify conditions associated with its occurrence

(3)　To suggest a plan for therapeutically removing the problem

(4)　To predict the probable outcome of this treatment

(5)　To predict the salient post-therapy behavior of the patient.

Phenotypic or behaviorally specific approaches will describe observable behavior, indicate the conditions which currently maintain it, plan intervention in terms of modifying these conditions, predict a change in the specific behavior patterns which have been treated—making few if any predictions about other behavioral changes. Genotypic or dispositional approaches will describe the inferential dynamics of the individual who emits the problem behavior, indicate the conditions presumably associated with its origin, plan intervention in terms of changing dynamics, and render generalized predictions of therapy and of post-therapy behavior.

The remainder of this chapter will be devoted to an analysis of the empirical evidence concerning genotypic diagnosis. A discussion of behavior assessment—phenotypic diagnosis—is reserved for Chapter 7. In this chapter, the term "dispositional diagnosis" will be used in order to stress the *pre*behavioral emphasis of the diagnosis. This generic term will be used to cover a broad range of diagnostic systems which differ in many important respects but which share a fundamental logic.

Psychiatric Classification: Reliability

The reliability of a psychiatric classification system can be meaningfully measured in two ways: by determining whether two or more judges rating the same patient will arrive at the same label, or by determining whether a patient will be given the same label when seen repeatedly for diagnostic purposes. The first type of reliability measure has been termed "inter-judge" reliability, while the second measure has been termed "test-retest" reliability.

The American Psychiatric Association (1952) has issued a nomenclature which has several hundred categories of adult psychopathology, and the Group for the Advancement of Psychiatry (1966) has issued a system for classifying the disorders of childhood which includes 10 major divisions with

58 subclassifications. The question which immediately presents itself when systems of this degree of complexity are discussed is whether well-trained clinicians can reliably apply the vast array of discriminations.

While some of the studies of the interjudge reliability of classification have yielded positive results (e. g., Foulds, 1955), it is more common for studies to show that very coarse categories such as "neurotic" or "psychotic" may be reliably applied, but reliability breaks down markedly when the finer categories are employed (Arnhoff, 1954; Ash, 1949; Boisen, 1938; Doering & Raymond, 1934; Eysenck, 1952; Hunt, Wittson & Hunt, 1953; Kanfer & Saslow, 1965; Kreitman, 1961; Kreitman, Sainsbury, Morrissey, Towers & Scrivener, 1961; Mehlman, 1952; Patrick, Overall & Tupin, 1968; Schmidt & Fonda, 1956). Negative results are also found in studies of test-retest reliability (Arthur & Gunderson, 1966; Kaelbling & Volpe, 1963), although this research is less common than research concerned with the agreement among clinicians.

A psychiatric diagnosis is typically the end product of a process of clinical judgment. In a general sense, the diagnosis is equal to the true characteristics of the patient plus the error or deviation of the observed score from the true score. Kogan (1959, p. 74) has represented this relationship with the following equation:

$$X = T + E$$

in which X is the observed rating, T is the patient's true characteristics and E is the difference between the observed and true scores. The sources of error are to be found in any of the major elements of the judgment situation, which include: individual characteristics of the clinician; individual characteristics of the patient; the type of judgment demanded, including the response alternatives which are available to the clinician; and the context or situation in which the judgments are made (Tripodi & Miller, 1966). The following sections will review each of these potential sources of error.

Individual characteristics of the clinician. In clinical assessment, the clinician usually interviews the patient and makes judgments about his behavior. It is obvious that different clinicians with differing expectations will ask different questions and therefore elicit different behavior in their patients. For example, a Freudian might ask about early life experiences, while a behaviorist is more likely to ask for descriptions of the current situation. These differences may be ascribed to the therapists' differing theoretical orientations. In addition, in response to their own personal orientations, therapists have been shown to elicit differing patterns of patient response. For example, it has been shown that some therapists (presumably those who are more comfortable with it) elicit patient hostility, while others (presumably less comfortable with it) withdraw from patient hostility (Bandura, Lipsher & Miller, 1960; Gamsky & Farwell, 1966; Mills & Abeles, 1965).

In addition to sampling different characteristics of patient behavior, clinicians are likely to interpret patient behavior in accordance with their own theoretical biases (Chapman & Chapman, 1967; Grosz & Grossman, 1968; C. Watson, 1967) or with personal idiosyncrasy mediated by personal definitions of commonly used descriptive terms (Bruner & Tagiuri, 1954; Elkin, 1947; Gordon, 1966; G. A. Kelly, 1955; Osgood, Suci & Tannenbaum, 1957).

Since diagnosis is the product of an interpersonal encounter, it is to be expected that some "human error" will enter into its outcome. Some of the errors may stem from the unplanned elicitation of patient responses, from inaccurate observation or from loose reasoning based upon such observations as are collected. Reasoning errors are perhaps the easiest to study and this may explain the relative volume of research in this area. It has been fairly well documented, for example, that clinicians are at times so personal in their criteria for the selection of certain diagnostic inferences that they are unable to offer a formal explanation for their choice (Gauron & Dickenson, 1966), while in other instances different clinicians have been shown to use very different criteria to support the use of the same diagnostic labels (Goldfarb, 1959; Mehlman, 1952; Thorne, 1961). Some educators have sought to correct these flaws through training which both has (Rotter, 1967) and has not (Mahrer, 1962) proven to be effective in overcoming these personal biases and/or idiocyncrasies. Because clinical judgment has been shown to be highly responsive to the characteristics of the clinician, it is of importance to study as carefully as possible how the characteristics of the clinician interact with his judgment output.

Holt and Luborsky (1958) have shown that there are wide variations in the reliability of the judgments rendered by particular clinicians, and other clinicians have supported the notion that a clinical judgment may reveal more about the clinician than it reveals about the patient whom he is judging (Kessel & Shepherd, 1962). Studies of this sort are based upon the collection of diagnoses made by several judges on numerous occasions. In one such investigation, Raines and Rohmer (1955) reviewed the judgments made by military psychiatrists in an effort to predict the suitability of officer trainees for command positions. It was shown that while the judgments tended to be accurate, marked differences appeared in the willingness of particular psychiatrists to use certain descriptive terms. For example, one psychiatrist might have a strong tendency to see depression in his patients while another psychiatrist might interpret the same behavior as sober and responsible; the first psychiatrist would refuse training to a candidate while the second would accept him, independent of the fact that his behavior may have been the same in both instances.

Some of the studies of clinician behavior have sought to relate the field of specialization of the clinical judge to his accuracy. In one review of the literature in this area (Sarbin, Taft & Bailey, 1960), it was shown that of 14 studies comparing the accuracy of psychologists and nonpsychologists, six showed no differences, five favored psychologists and three favored nonpsychologists. Typical of the research are studies which compare the accuracy of psychologists with the accuracy of physical scientists, often to the embarrassment of the psychologists (Luft, 1950; Taft, 1955; Weiss, 1962). Even in studies in which nonsignificant differences are found between clinicians and nonclinicians, it is not uncommon to find that individual laymen (e. g., Protestant housewives) outperform psychologists (Cline, 1955). This calls attention to the role of the experience of the clinical judge. While most studies in this area demonstrate that experience does not enhance reliability (Brieland, 1959; Grigg, 1958; Sarbin, Taft & Bailey, 1960; Soskin, 1959), other studies show that it may aid judgments under some circumstances (R. R. Miller, 1958) but it may actually decrease inter-rater reliability in other circumstances (Arnhoff, 1954; Crow, 1957).

Another line of investigation in this area has shown that the cognitive characteristics of the clinician can materially affect his judgment. For example, Plotnick (1961) showed that judges who were more extraceptive (i. e., more impersonal and objective) in their approaches were more accurate than clinicians who were introceptive (i. e., warmer and more subjective). This finding may in part account for the general superiority of physical scientists as compared to clinical psychologists in judgment studies. In another series of studies, G. A. Kelly's (1955) Role Construct Repertory Test has been used to differentiate cognitively complex judges from cognitively noncomplex judges. Cognitive complexity refers to several abilities including: (a) the capacity to generate several different ways to classify the same phenomenon; (b) the capacity to use these differing classifications as a means of increasing the precision of observations and as a means of organizing these observations in a manner which reflects differing nuances of the phenomenon; and (c) the capacity to reconcile apparently contradictory observations in assessing a particular phenomenon. These characteristics were then intercorrelated with judgment performance and resulted in the disclosures that cognitively complex judges were more alert to conflict in the data which they were asked to judge (Tripodi, 1967; Tripodi & Bieri, 1966), were able to include a greater amount of more varied data in their judgments (Tripodi & Bieri, 1964) and tended to be more accurate in their judgments (Plotnick, 1961).

In light of these various lines of investigation, it can be concluded that clinical judgment is a process which is highly sensitive to the characteristics of the clinician. One clinician may view a patient as relatively healthy, while a second clinician interviewing the same patient may view him as deeply disturbed. The differences in the assessment are more likely to be a product of honest disagreement than chicanery. But in order to reduce the likelihood of such disagreements, interview situations should be standardized, clinicians should be comparably trained and the tasks set before clinicians should be as objective as is possible.

Individual characteristics of the patient. Clinical judgment typically occurs through an interpersonal process. It goes without saying that if the characteristics of the clinician influence the judgment outcome, the characteristics of the client must surely contribute importantly to this outcome. In theory, the clinician bases his judgment solely on the behavior of his patient. In practice, factors other than client behavior may materially affect the judgment outcome. For example, there have been consistent findings that the socioeconomic status of the patient has a direct bearing upon the severity ascribed to his pathology. This finding has been supported through two lines of investigation.

Demographic studies have shown that lower-class patients are far more likely to receive severely pathological diagnoses for conditions which are diagnosed as less severe in middle-class patients (Hollingshead & Redlich, 1958; McDermott, Harrison, Schrager & Wilson, 1965; Pasamanick, Roberts, Lemkau & Krueger, 1964). In another line of investigation reviewed by Stuart (1965), clinicians were asked to judge a series of paired written descriptions of clients, which were identical except for reference to socioeconomic class. It was shown that class factors were strongly influential in decisions about the suitability of prospective adoptive parents (Borgatta, Fanshel & Meyer, 1960), the degree of personality disturbance of prospective clients (Briar, 1961a, 1961b), and the nature of social work treatment that would be offered to clients who are accepted for service (Rice, 1963).

If class factors are of such great importance, it would be unreasonable to exclude the possibility that other patient characteristics such as race, nationality and manner of speech might also be of importance. For example, in some instances persons are likely to give a much higher rating to others whom they perceive to be like themselves or whom they like. In addition, some studies have shown that judgments tend to be more critical or differentiating when negative affect is ascribed to the person being judged (Irwin, Tripodi & Bieri, 1967; R. Turner & Tripodi, 1968).

One final set of client characteristics that may be influential in determining the conclusions drawn about the client are his attitudes towards being examined or tested (Wilcox & Krasnoff, 1967). Both the motivation of the respondent (Heron, 1956) and his general tendency to say "yes" or "no" (Couch & Kenniston, 1960) may influence his test results. Furthermore, people have differing tendencies to say what is socially desirable (Edwards & Walsh, 1964) or to seek the approval of others (Crowne & Marlowe, 1964), and these behaviors might lead to a persuasive increment or decrement in the extent to which an individual is positively evaluated. The reward for these acquiescent responses may well be acceptance into a treatment program (Denzin, 1968), but their effect is clearly harmful to the accuracy of clinical judgment. It can therefore be concluded that many characteristics of the patient may contribute to judgments made about him, despite the fact that a number of these characteristics have no direct bearing upon the formal decisions that are being made.

Types and alternatives of clinical judgment. Since the clinical judgment process is very sensitive to characteristics of the clinician and some irrelevant characteristics of the patient, it is essential that the required judgment be based upon a cogent and explicit logic and that it be structured in a manner which enhances the probability of accuracy.

The currently used American Psychiatric Association (1952) diagnostic classification does not provide such an aid, as it suffers from four major structural weaknesses. First, the system is deductively derived from assumptions about clinical pathology rather than inductively derived from direct observation of such pathology. This problem has been characterized by Rubin (1948) as an effort to use Aristotelian rather than Galilean logic, which results in the postulation of entities which cannot be shown to exist. Second, the system is composed of a bewildering array of categories which seeks to anticipate every conceivable configuration rather than to stress primarily those entities that are commonly observed. This has resulted in a system of such complexity as to defy the possibility that it can be reliably applied. Third, great disagreement exists about the definition and implication of some of the general categories. For example, the problem of "schizophrenia" has been viewed as subject to very widely differing assessment (R. C. Hunt & Appel, 1936; Langfeldt, 1951), probably more accurately reflecting a continuum of problems (Kantor & Herron, 1966), and subject to widely differing inferences ranging from organic to psychogenic origin, from curability to incurability, from a need to stress psychodynamics to a need to avoid psychodynamics, and from a stress upon qualitative divergences from normalcy to a stress upon quantitative divergence from normalcy (Rumke, 1960).

The fourth structural weakness in the diagnostic system is inherent in the fact that it is premised upon the belief that patterns of behavior systematically covary such that when one response of a pattern is observed, the presence of the others can be inferred. To be reliable, such a system must consist of mutually exclusive behavioral families, for when behavioral families overlap, multiple predictions would be warranted. In clinical terms, this aspect of a diagnostic system is measured by determining whether "pathognomonic cues" are available to indicate the relevance of one and only one category (Thorne, 1961). It must be concluded that the dispositional (Kraepelinean) system currently in use lacks these cues (Freudenberg & Robertson, 1956; Kreitman, Sainsbury, Morrissey, Towers & Scrivener, 1961; Wittenborn, 1952; Wittenborn & Bailey, 1952; Wittenborn, Holzberg & Simon, 1953; Wittenborn & Weiss, 1952). The general conclusion of these varied studies can be summarized by the following statement.

> A certain degree of relationship has been discovered between symptom manifestation and diagnosis. However, the most striking finding of the present study is that the magnitude of these relationships is generally so small that membership in a particular diagnostic group conveys only minimal information about the symptomatology of the patient. One is faced with the perplexing finding that the occurrence of a wide variety of symptoms may be related to more than one diagnostic category [Zigler & Phillips, 1961a, p. 73].

In light of this array of evidence, one must conclude that Rotter's (1954) view that symptoms are completely chance occurrences unrelated to deeper and more dynamic aspects of individual functioning has received important, if not conclusive, support.

Following an appraisal of the logic of the category system, it is important to review the effect which such a multidimensional system may have upon the judgments that result from its application. The system calls for an impressive array of data, but it has been shown in many studies that an increase in the amount of information brought to bear upon particular decisions may not enhance the accuracy of these decisions (Borke & Fiske, 1957; Cline, 1955; Daily, 1952; Kostlan, 1954; Sines, 1959). In studies of the effect of increasing information, two general questions can be raised.

First, it may be asked whether an increase in the amount of information offered along a single dimension enhances the accuracy of judgment. Bieri (1962) studied the effect of increases in the amount of unidimensional information given to social work students and found that judgments were altered as a consequence of whether one to four bits of information were made available, but judgments were not changed as the amount of information progressed from four to eight bits. This result is reflected in two studies of the clinical judgment process coincident with psychotherapy which reveal that clinicians reach an early appraisal of their patients and do not modify these impressions as treatment progresses (Meehl, 1960; Parker, 1958).

The second question that may be asked is whether the addition of new dimensions of information enhances the judgment outcome. Studies addressing this problem have shown that psychiatrists, psychologists and social workers can make more accurate judgments based upon either the sound or visual content of motion pictures than they can make when both data sources are available (Giedt, 1955), while predictions about the performance of graduate students in psychology were as accurate on the basis of biographic material and objective tests as were predictions based upon interviews, comprehensive testing, and autobiographical material (E. L. Kelly & Fiske, 1951).

If increased information does not enhance the accuracy of clinical judgment, one may wonder if it has a decremental effect upon accuracy. Several studies have shown that in fact there is an inverse relationship between the amount of information and the accuracy of judgment (Cline & Richards, 1960; Dymond, 1953; Hathaway, 1956; Huff, 1966; Leventhal, 1957; Sawyer, 1966; Schwartz, 1967). While this supposition can be qualified by the notion that redundant information may impede the reliability of judgment at the same time that new information increases reliability (Huff & Friedman, 1967), other researchers argue that increased information may lead to an inappropriate ascription of relevance (E. L. Kelly & Fiske, 1950). It is argued that first-order relations between predictors and criteria are given up in favor of less dependable higher order relations when the amount of information becomes vast (Estes, 1957).

In summary, it must be realized that the clinician has a finite and perhaps quite limited capacity for processing information (Bieri, Atkins, Briar, Leaman, Miller & Tripodi, 1966; G. A. Miller, 1956; H. Miller & Bieri, 1963; Tripodi & Bieri, 1964). Peterson (1965), for example, has argued that

> . . .most of the initially obscure, apparently more precise, more narrowly defined factors many investigators claim to have revealed are either trivial, artifactual, capricious, or all 3. Verbal descriptions of personality were reduced to 2 factors, and the 2 factors were reduced to 2 ratings, 1 concerning perceived adjustment and the other related to introversion-extraversion [p. 48].

If all of the refinement in psychiatric categorization does not enhance the reliability of clinical judgments, and if the multidimensional category system is further weakened by a faulty logical structure, then there appears to be at best a guarded hope that studies of the reliability of these judgments might reach a criterion level of acceptability.

The context in which clinical judgments are made. A fourth factor which might contribute to the low reliability of dispositional diagnosis is its sensitivity to aspects of the situation in which it is derived. Many studies can be cited in support of the contention that diagnosis represents an interaction of situation X therapist X client (Moos & Clemes, 1967). One important characteristic is the nature of the test situation itself. For example, it has been shown that among culturally deprived nursery school children who underwent group intelligence testing, those who were individually retested immediately showed a greater improvement in scores than those who were retested on a group basis following an entire year of nursery school (Zigler & Butterfield, 1968). (The importance of a year of nursery school is suggested by

B. S. Bloom's [1964] observation that children acquire over 50 per cent of their adult [age 18] intelligence by the age of five.)

Characteristics of the person administering the test are an additional source of variance in test responses (Masling, 1960; Mechanic, 1962). The behavior of the tester is important because he is both an initiator and evaluator of patients' responses (Garfield, 1963). As an illustration, it has been shown that brain-damaged subjects test at higher levels of perceptual-motor functioning when exposed to interested rather than disinterested interview procedures (Parsons & Stewart, 1966; see also Gravitz & Handler, 1968).

An additional source of error is the effect which the testing situation can have upon the test-taking set or attitude of the person who is being examined. Set refers to a generalized predisposition to respond and predisposition in testing situations may be subject to influence by the examiner. For example, Kroger (1968) showed that subjects could be instructed to respond "as though" they possessed a particular constellation of characteristics with the result that wide variation could be introduced into their responses. While it is unlikely that examiners would intentionally mislead examinees, it seems likely that more subtle cues in their behavior can affect examinee responses.

In summary, it can be said that psychiatric diagnosis and clinical judgments which in general depend upon the identification of dispositional characteristics in the patient have not demonstrated a high level of reliabilty. The lack of reliability can be attributed in part to weaknesses in the conception of the diagnostic typologies and in part is intrinsic in the situations in which judgments are made. The complexity and generality of the problems would seem to indicate a clear need to develop alternative modes of client assessment which would tend to be more free of potential error.

Psychiatric Diagnosis: Validity

Validity is concerned with the extent to which an instrument is useful in fulfilling the purpose for which it was intended. The American Psychological Association (1954) has identified four types of validity. Two of the types of validity (content and construct) are concerned with whether the instrument measures what it is expected to measure and whether it is closely tied to explicit explanatory constructs. The two remaining measures of validity are classed as statistical or empirical measures and are concerned with the degree to which the instrument can be used to predict the patient's future behavior or to predict his behavior in other concurrent situations. The major interest of the clinician is in the predictions which he can safely make from his observations, and therefore this section will stress data pertinent to statistical validity.

Dispositional diagnosis as a predictor of type of treatment. If diagnosis is conceived to be a prescription for some action rather than a description of the patient (Linder, 1965), then it is appropriate to evaluate diagnosis in terms of the accuracy with which it predicts the nature of the service to be offered. Generally, it can be concluded that dispositional diagnostic systems do not predict which treatment will be undertaken (Coles & Magnussen, 1966; Kanfer & Saslow, in press). An early investigation (Dailey, 1953) showed that clinical reports make a difference only 26 per cent of the time. A later study of 132 clinicians (Meehl, 1960) revealed that while 17 per cent of the clinicians studied felt that prior knowledge of the patient was important in effective treatment, 80 per cent felt that therapist characteristics are important determinants of the nature of treatment offered and its outcome, and 40 per cent felt that even incorrect interpretations not even near the actual facts could have real and long-lasting therapeutic effects. Another study of the attitude of psychologists toward the usefulness of testing also showed that 65-75 per cent of those asked responded that psychological test report data had no relevance to therapeutic decision-making (Mintz, 1968). One of the more careful and comprehensive studies (Bannister, Salmon & Leiberman, 1964) found that treatment could be accurately predicted in gross terms from gross diagnoses while more precise diagnoses fell far short of this in predicting precise treatment techniques.

There are several explanations for this result. First, it can be hypothesized that the range of diagnostic types far exceeds the range of relevant therapeutic alternatives, so that the complexity of the diagnostic information may exceed the range of treatment techniques (Lakin & Lieberman, 1965). Thus while it might be possible to identify a myriad of sub-types of neurosis (Fenichel, 1945), there may be but a single therapeutic alternative. Second, it can be hypothesized that the categories of dispositional diagnosis are at best loosely linked to alternative courses of therapeutic action (Breger, 1968; Coles & Magnussen, 1966). As an example, client-centered therapy has developed a measure of self-concept while psychoanalysis has developed a morphology of character types. Thus it can be assumed that, to the extent that these diagnostic systems do not merely imply different labels for the same phenomenon, each set of descriptive terms should lead to a different treatment strategy. However, the conclusion of one recent investigation was:

> Actually, the range of verbal behaviors open to psychoanalytic and client-centered therapists is not so very different given the goals they are pursuing; and since the goals for both types of treatment have a good deal in common, the results of this study should not be surprising [R. D. Cartwright, 1966, p. 527].

It would appear, then, that despite the variance in the content and structure of the diagnostic systems in these two schools of therapy, the treatment offered to patients may not be very different (Eysenck, 1965, p. 104). This would support the hypothesis that dispositional diagnosis may be at best loosely linked to treatment.

The suggestion that a treatment typology is not logically implied by the dispositional diagnostic typologies can be extended into yet a third explanation of the low validity of the diagnostic system: The terms of diagnosis may be essentially irrelevant to treatment (Zigler & Phillips, 1961b)—that is, they may make "no practical contribution to treatment [Breger, 1968, p. 178]"—just as they are irrelevant to decision-making in institutional settings (Street, Vinter & Perrow, 1966).

If the goals of psychotherapy are essentially reconstructive (Lorr & McNair, 1966), then it would seem imperative that diagnosis stress the strengths upon which improved functioning must be premised (Martin, 1966; Scarbrough, 1966). Quite to the contrary, however, dispositional nosologies appear to be heavily overbalanced by referents to pathology (Leifer, 1964; Sarbin, 1967), with normalcy construed as the absence of pathology (Garfield, 1963), and even the absence of pathological responses may be regarded as pathological defensiveness (Skolnick, 1966).

Just as clinical vocabulary is heavily pathology-oriented, so too are clinicians likely to emit clinical judgments that are heavily skewed in the direction of pathology (Little & Shneidman, 1959; Weiss, 1963). For example, Stuart (1968) asked 106 professional social workers to list adjectives describing persons who were normal or abnormal, psychologically healthy or psychologically ill. The group produced an average of 3.01 descriptors of healthy individuals and 12.73 descriptors of unhealthy individuals. In a more systematic series of studies (Lakin & Lieberman, 1965; Soskin, 1954, 1959), clinicians were asked first to rate a patient following minimal information describing his behavior and situation and then to rate him after receiving dispositional data. As predicted, both groups of clinicians moved dramatically from positive to negative evaluations following the availability of nonbehavioral descriptions.

It is possible to relate this pathology focus of clinicians to their adherence to the medical model which was discussed in

Chapter 1. One of the dicta of the physician is "When in doubt, diagnose illness" (Scheff, 1963). Whatever the explanation of the phenomenon, however, it must be evident that the overemphasis on observations of pathology can only help to dampen both patient and therapist expectancy of success, to introduce a very skewed bias in the sampling of behavior which is discussed in treatment, and to reinforce negative goals (removal of pathology) in place of the positive goals (promotion of adaptive functioning) which would be more appropriate therapeutic objectives.

Dispositional diagnosis as a predictor of behavior during and after treatment. If dispositional diagnosis does not predict the type of treatment to be offered, it is reasonable to ask whether it will at least predict the outcome of whatever treatment should happen to materialize. Strong evidence supports a negative result in this area, whether the treatment is psychotherapy (D. S. Cartwright, Kirtner & Fiske, 1963; Small, Saunders, Small & Morton, 1967), psychiatric hospitalization (Arthur & Gunderson, 1966; Brink, Oetting & Cole, 1967; Brown, Carstairs & Topping, 1958), or incarceration (Gough, Wenk & Rozynko, 1965; Schuessler & Cressey, 1950; Waldo & Dinitz, 1967; Wirt & Briggs, 1959).

One provocative study concluded that less than 10 per cent of the variance of factors contributing to the length of stay of mental patients in hospitals could be ascribed to psychopathology (R. J. Turner & Cumming, 1967, p. 50, n. 2). The obvious explanation for this and the findings cited earlier is that there are other factors which are far more important to decision making than psychopathology. One such factor is surely situational or demographic characteristics which have been identified as highly reliable predictors of post-psychiatric institutional behavior (Johnston & McNeal, 1967; Lindemann, Fairweather, Stone, Smith & London, 1959) and of parole behavior (Gough, Wenk & Rozynko, 1965; Smith & Lanyon, 1968).

One way to view the importance of situational characteristics is to review some of the specific findings in follow-up research. For example, Freeman and Simmons (1963) found that the ability of an ex-mental patient to remain in the community depended upon an interaction of his symptomatic responses and work behavior with whether he lived with his parents or spouse. A similar conclusion was drawn from the data collected by Dinitz, Lefton, Angrist and Pasamanick (1961), who found that:

> The seemingly best post-hospital functioners are married women, of relatively high socioeconomic class status, residing in nuclear households, having relatively young children, and without other adult females to serve as role replacements. It is helpful, too, if they have been diagnosed as non-organic but it makes little difference whether they are classed as psychotic or non-psychotic [p. 324].

In addition to such specific factors as family configuration and the behavioral expectancies of key members of the community, social class has been shown to have a powerful effect upon treatment outcome. Because class factors have been found to be associated with the occurrence of problems, it is not surprising to find that even though some lower-class patients might show clinical improvement during the course of treatment, these gains are not sustained when the patients return to their preinstitutional homes (McPartland & Richart, 1966).

In addition, the finding that individuals, settings and modes of response combine to account for the variance of treatment outcome (Moos, 1968) lends support to the position advocated by Szasz (1960), among others, that "mental illness" may be a social disease rather than a psychological disease. Indeed, if the correlations between illness, outcome and situational factors continue to receive support, those who stress the etiological significance of psychological characteristics will be in very much the same position as the social Darwinists, who almost eighty years ago sought to explain poverty in terms of moral inferiority (Hofstadter, 1955).

A general summary of the reliability and validity of the psychiatric nomenclature which is based upon dispositional

diagnosis must stress the fact that the reliability and validity
of this system have not been established. This is in no sense a
final judgment, as reformulations of the typology and more
effective training of clinicians in its use may overcome some
of the faults that have been identified. On the other hand, the
existence of these serious limitations should serve as a clear
warning to clinicians that extreme care must be exercised
when clinical diagnoses are rendered.

Projective Psychological Tests

At least some of the faults which limit the utility of the
clinical diagnostic system may be related to the relative lack
of standardization of the type of data collected, or to the
interpretations that are applied to these data. Psychological
testing offers one method of controlling the elicitation and
interpretation of patient responses, and therefore an examination of test results may offer the most critical test of the
reliability and validity of dispositional diagnosis.

Projective tests differ from psychometric tests in many
ways (Pope & Scott, 1967, pp. 113-120). First, projective tests
such as the Rorschach, Thematic Apperception, and Draw-a-
Person tests present stimuli which are ambiguous in meaning,
while psychometric tests such as the Wechsler Adult Intelligence Scale present stimuli which are precise in meaning.
The ambiguity of the projective tests is designed to give the
examinee the widest possible latitude in his responses, which
are believed to be more self-revealing as a result. A second
difference between projective and psychometric tests is the
extent of the chains of inference from patient's response to
examiner's conclusions. From explanations of ink blots,
Rorschach testers seek to infer behavioral potentials, while
intelligence testers, with greater economy of inference, reason
from arithmetic responses to I.Q. ratings.

A third difference between the two tests concerns the
mode of scoring. Projective tests are scored on the basis of

the examiner's evaluation of the inner meaning which the examinee "projects" into his responses, while the psychometric responses are, at least initially, taken at face value to be direct indications of the patient's characteristics in the areas under study. As a caution, however, it should be clearly indicated that it may be "mythical to think of a coherent generalized category of 'projective tests' [Fisher, 1967]," so overextended generalizations may be hazardous.

It can be said that the accuracy of judgments based upon projective test data appears to be low. For example, Chambers and Hamlin (1957) asked experienced clinicians to differentiate the Rorschach responses of involutional depressives, anxiety neurotics, paranoid schizophrenics, adult paretics and mental defectives. The judges succeeded in differentiating the responses of the adult imbeciles but were right only half of the time with the remaining patients. Other experimenters have shown that clinicians using the Rorschach will be completely wrong at least one in five times (Garfield, 1947; Michael & Buhler, 1945; Payne, 1958). Even when Rorschach test results are confirmed, however, Cronbach (1949) observed that the statistical procedures of the positive research are so poor as to invalidate the results. He said: "Perhaps ninety percent of the conclusions so far published as a result of statistical Rorschach studies are unsubstantiated [p. 425]."

The same general low level of reliabiltiy is found when the Draw-a-Person (DAP) test (Machover, 1949) is employed. It has been estimated that this test is the second most widely used projective test in American hospitals and clinics (Sundberg, 1961). Swensen (1957) reviewed the evidence drawn from research conducted during the first eight years that the test was in general use. He concluded that the clinical usefulness of the instrument was not demonstrated. Wanderer, in 1964, completed a definitive study using the DAP. He assembled a group of 25 clinicians who were nominated and ranked by their peers as the foremost experts in the use of the test. He presented them with one pair of drawings produced by one subject from each of five criterion groups ranging from mental defectives to neurotics. The experts were asked to assign a rank-ordered probability to each drawing from each category. Thus an expert might indicate that the greatest probability was that a particular drawing was the product of a defective, that a psychotic was second most likely to have produced that drawing, etc. Wanderer's (1966) conclusion was:

> The judges' successes were compared with those expected by chance. It was found that experts using the DAP alone are capable of identifying mental defectives far beyond chance expectations. The four remaining groups, however, were found not to be identifiable by means of the DAP, even in the hands of experts, and even after the experts are permitted a second chance to make a correct diagnosis [p. 67].

Moving into the area of validity studies, it can be shown that methodological errors plague the studies that reach affirmative conclusions. For example, Chambers and Hamlin (1957) showed that Rorschach test results correlated with clinical diagnosis, but the test protocols were presented to subjects as part of a patient folder which contained other biasing information. A similar error was found in Wallon's (1959) validation of the DAP. Another error which is not uncommon was illustrated by Holzberg and Wexler (1950) in their effort to validate the DAP. Their subjects successfully differentiated nursing students from schizophrenic women, but the students were all younger than the patients and age has been shown to have a marked bearing upon DAP results (Lorge, Tuckman & Dunn, 1954). A third error was found by Meehl (1965) in the work of Lindzey (1965). Lindzey demonstrated that clinicians could identify homosexual college students from nonhomosexual students on the basis of responses to the Thematic Apperception Test, but Meehl indicated that stylistic features of the test protocol rather than theoretically relevant variables accounted for a major portion of the result.

Some of the major efforts to validate projective tests have been concerned with showing their association with each other, with psychiatric diagnosis or with some other behavioral variable such as employment or academic achievement. There are two serious qualifications which must be recognized in connection with these efforts. First, the reliability of psychiatric diagnosis itself rarely exceeds .70, which means that its correlation with any other variable cannot exceed this level (Inglis, 1966, p. 9). Second, the logic of the test procedure itself must be explicit if the test results are to be used properly. Despite this fact, it is common practice to validate psychological tests solely or primarily against psychiatric diagnosis (Payne, 1958). Third, Johnson (1928) has indicated that a " 'test' is an indirect means of measuring an empirical and variable quantity [p. 329]" and that, in order to use a test for scientific purposes, both the test and the behavior with which it is being correlated must be capable of independent measurement and their interrelationship must be specifiable. There is no set of projective tests which meets these criteria.

When projective tests are intercorrelated, it is shown that some inter-test agreements occur among tests of the same type (Dana, 1962) but that agreement between tests of different types is very small (Fisher, 1967; Goldberg & Werts, 1966; Lipsher, 1962; Mogar, 1962). Anticipation of these results undoubtedly motivated Rapaport and Schafer (1946, p. 98) in their classic manual on testing to caution clinicians about making judgments based upon responses to a single test. In addition to shedding doubt upon the intercorrelation among tests, the research literature also contains some negative findings with respect to the contribution of test data to the accuracy of clinical diagnosis (Kostlan, 1954; Sines, 1957) and with respect to the relationship between test responses and social functioning (Fulkerson & Barry, 1961). As an example of the research in the latter area, Lowe (1967) collected Rorschach, Minnesota Multiphasic Personality Inventory and Wechsler Adult Intelligence Scale data on patients who had been discharged from a mental hospital. Of 39 possible intercorrelations, only three scales were significantly associated with vocational success: Popular responses on the Rorschach, MMPI K score responses, and Block Design scores on the WAIS. Furthermore, the significance of even these scores disappears in the cross-validating sample, leading Lowe to conclude:

> While these three most frequently used tests. . .may have been quite useful in terms of making a traditional type of diagnostic evaluation and may still be very important for matters involving personality theory and research, they seem to be of only limited utility in treatment programs where psychologists are involved with others in a program of behavioral modification which uses as its criterion successful future vocational adjustment in the community [p. 252].

Accepting the caution that there are, as yet, few fully documented facts in psychology (Shneidman, 1959), the clinician who would use projective tests must answer Meehl's (1954) question, "Am I doing better than I could do by flipping pennies [p. 136]?" An honest answer to this question must be a qualified "no." Almost 25 years ago, W. A. Hunt (1946) suggested that the field of psychological testing was in need of revitalization through careful research. He said:

> Psychological testing has firmly established itself as a diagnostic procedure in clinical practice. The tests employed and the diagnostic uses to which they are put are well known and it is not proposed to review them here. Rather let us face the disturbing fact that diagnostic testing is at present in a state of relative stagnation. Anyone surveying the tremendous development of clinical psychology during the last ten years, and the major importance that psychological testing assumes in such clinical practice, cannot help but be struck by the small amount of progress we have made in developing our psychological tests as diagnostic instruments. Our advances have been in the expansion of physical facilities, in the extension of clinical services, rather than in the improvement of our existing diagnostic techniques and the discovery of new ones [p. 311].

This state of affairs still existed 13 years later, leading Little (1959) to state:

> It is somewhat embarrassing to have to say that the published evidence on projective techniques indicates that they have either zero or, at best, very low positive effective validity indices. Even in those studies with the most positive results, correlations are of an order of magnitude which make predictions for the individual largely a waste of time.
>
> This distressing state of affairs has been with us unchanged for a rather long period of time. . .The only noticeable change has been in the sophistication of design and analysis. Negative or ambiguous results, however, are just as disheartening when determined by an F ratio as when determined by a critical ratio [p. 287].

It is possible to ascribe the persistent stagnation in the field of projective testing to the unscientific attitudes of vocal clinicians in that field. For example, in response to Swensen's (1957) critique of the DAP, Hammer (1959) wrote:

> In the face of a complex world, the research worker is obligated to recognize the complexity of the variables he attempts to come to grips with in his investigations, and steer vigorously away from the dangers of *atomistic studies, naively conceived and dogmatically interpreted* [p. 32, italics mine].

As another example, Klopfer, Ainsworth, Klopfer and Holt (1954) asserted:

> . . .all these 'blind' interpretations and diagnoses seem to be more of a *tour de force* to impress the skeptic than to represent a serious attempt to test out the basic hypotheses upon which interpretation and diagnosis are based [p. 463].

As long as these responses to valid criticism persist, the field of projective testing will not undergo the critical self-corrective process required if it is to retain any vestige of a scientific mantle. Instead, it is apparent that at least some of the outspoken proponents of projective testing are content to rely upon mere definition of their salient variables, often supported by methodologically unsound research, in contrast to developing rigorous operational meanings for components of the language of diagnosis.

Summary

After differentiating phenotypic from genotypic diagnosis, an extensive array of evidence has been reviewed in this chapter in support of the notion that genotypic, or dispositional, diagnoses have a high probability of unreliability and invalidity. These findings were not in themselves surprising, as it is reasonable to expect that the assessment of an unobservable entity must be a highly variable procedure. What is surprising, on the other hand, is the apparent complacency with which the mental health profession has accepted such discordant results. The same criticisms have been expressed in similar terms for years. Yet practitioners continue to use the same unproductive procedures, ignoring the principle that scientists must constantly correct their methods in the light of experience.

In the next chapter it will be shown that the ineffective diagnostic practices are potentially quite harmful to the patients who receive pathological labels. The need to correct faulty procedures is therefore not an academic matter but rather a matter of vital necessity if the interests of patients and the scientific character of the mental health professions are to be protected.

References

American Psychiatric Association. *Diagnostic and statistical manual of mental disorders.* Washington, D.C.: American Psychiatric Association, 1952.

American Psychological Association. Technical recommendations for psychological tests and diagnostic techniques. *Psychological Bulletin Supplement,* 1954, 51(1).

Arnhoff, F. N. Some factors influencing the unreliability of clinical judgments. *Journal of Clinical Psychology,* 1954, 10, 272-275.

Arthur, R. J. & Gunderson, E. K. E. The prediction of diagnosis and disposition in naval hospitals. *Journal of Clinical Psychology,* 1966, 22, 259-264.

Ash, P. The reliability of psychiatric diagnosis. *Journal of Abnormal and Social Psychology,* 1949, 44, 272-276.

Bandura, A., Lipsher, D. H. & Miller, P. Psychotherapists' approach-avoidance reactions to patients' expressions of hostility. *Journal of Consulting Psychology,* 1960, 24, 1-8.

Bannister, D., Salmon, P. & Leiberman, D. M. Diagnosis-treatment relationships in psychiatry: A statistical analysis. *British Journal of Psychiatry,* 1964, 110, 726-732.

Barrett, B. H. & Lindsley, O. R. Deficits in acquisition of operant discrimination and differentiation shown by institutionalized retarded children. *American Journal of Mental Deficiency,* 1962, 67, 424-436.

Bieri, J. Analyzing stimulus information in social judgments. In S. Messick & J. Ross (Eds,), *Measurement in personality and cognition.* New York: Wiley, 1962. Pp 229-240.

Bieri, J., Atkins, A. L., Briar, S., Leaman, R. L., Miller, H. & Tripodi, T. *Clinical and social judgment.* New York: Wiley, 1966.

Bloom, B. S. *Stability and change in human characteristics.* New York: Wiley, 1964.

Boisen, A. T. Types of dementia praecox–a study in psychiatric classification. *Psychiatry,* 1938, 1, 233-236.

Borgatta, E. F., Fanshel, D., & Meyer, H. J. *Social workers' perceptions of their clients.* New York: Russell Sage Foundation, 1960.

Borke, H. & Fiske, D. W. Factors influencing the prediction of behavior from a diagnostic interview. *Journal of Consulting Psychology,* 1957, 21, 78-80.

Breger, L. Psychological testing: Treatment and research implications. *Journal of Consulting and Clinical Psychology,* 1968, 32, 176-181.

Briar, S. The effects of clients' social class, social class distance and social work experience in the judgments of social work students. Unpublished doctoral dissertation, Columbia University School of Social Work, 1961. (a)

Briar, S. The use of theory in studying effects of client social class on students' judgments. *Social Work,* 1961, 6(3), 91-97. (b)

Brieland, D. *An experimental study of the selection of adoptive parents at intake.* New York: Child Welfare League of America, 1959.

Brink, R. W., Oetting, E. R. & Cole, C. W. Technical research report number X: Predicting post-hospital outcome of psychiatric patients. Unpublished manuscript, Mental Health and Manpower Project, Colorado State University, 1967.

Brown, G. W., Carstairs, G. M. & Topping, G. Post-hospital adjustment of chronic mental patients. *The Lancet,* 1958, 2, 685-689.

Bruner, J. S. & Tagiuri, R. The perception of people. In G. Lindzey, *Handbook of social psychology: Special fields and applications,* Vol. 2. Reading, Mass.: Addison-Wesley, 1954. Pp. 634-654.

Cartwright, D. S., Kirtner, W. L. & Fiske, D. W. Method factors in changes associated with psychotherapy. *Journal of Abnormal and Social Psychology,* 1963, 66, 164-175.

Cartwright, R. D. A comparison of the response to psychoanalytic and client-centered psychotherapy. In L. A. Gottschalk & A. Auerbach, *Methods of research in psychotherapy.* New York: Appleton-Century-Crofts, 1966.

Chambers, G. S. & Hamlin, R. M. The validity of judgments based on "blind" Rorschach records. *Journal of Consulting Psychology,* 1957, 21, 105-109.

Chapman, L. & Chapman, J. Genesis of popular but erroneous psychodiagnostic observations. *Journal of Abnormal Psychology,* 1967, 72, 193-204.

Cline, V. B. Ability to judge personality assessed with a stress interview and sound-film technique. *Journal of Abnormal and Social Psychology,* 1955, 50, 183-187.

Cline, V. B. & Richards, J. M., Jr. The accuracy of interpersonal perception: A general trait? *Journal of Abnormal and Social Psychology,* 1960, 60, 1-7.

Coles, J. K. & Magnussen, M. G. Where the action is. *Journal of Consulting Psychology,* 1966, 30, 539-543.

Couch, A. S. & Keniston, K. Yeasayers and naysayers: Agreeing response set as a personality variable. *Journal of Abnormal and Social Psychology,* 1960, 60, 151-174.

Cronbach, L. J. Statistical methods applied to Rorschach scores: A review. *Psychological Bulletin,* 1949, 46, 393-429.

Crow, W. J. The effect of training upon accuracy and variability in interpersonal perception. *Journal of Abnormal and Social Psychology,* 1957, 55, 355-359.

Dailey, C. A. The effects of premature conclusions upon the acquisition of understanding of a person. *Journal of Psychology,* 1952, 33, 133-152.

Dailey, C. A. Practical utility of the clinical report. *Journal of Consulting Psychology,* 1953, 17, 297-302.

Dana, R. H. The validation of projective tests. *Journal of Projective Techniques,* 1962, 26, 182-186.

Denzin, N. K. The self-fulfilling prophesy and patient-therapist interaction. In S. P. Spitzer & N. K. Denzin (Eds.), *The mental patient: Studies in the sociology of deviance.* New York: McGraw-Hill, 1968. Pp. 349-358.

Dinitz, S., Lefton, M., Angrist, S. & Pasamanick, B. Psychiatric and social attributes as predictors of case outcome in mental hospitalization. *Social Problems,* 1961, 8, 322-328.

Doering, C. R. & Raymond, A. F. Reliability of observation in psychiatric and related characteristics. *American Journal of Orthopsychiatry,* 1934, 4, 249-257.

Dymond, R. F. Can clinicians predict individual behavior? *Journal of Personality,* 1953, 22, 151-161.

Edwards, A. L. & Walsh, J. A. Response sets in standard and experimental personality scales. *American Educational Research Journal,* 1964, 1, 52-60.

Elkin, F. Specialists interpret the case of Harold Holzer. *Journal of Abnormal and Social Psychology,* 1947, 42, 99-111.

Estes, W. K. Of models and men. *American Psychologist,* 1957, 12, 609-617.

Eysenck, H. J. *The scientific study of personality.* London: Routledge & Kegan Paul, 1952.

Eysenck, H. J. The effects of psychotherapy. *International Journal of Psychiatry,* 1965, 1, 97-144.

Fenichel, O. *The psychoanalytic theory of neurosis.* New York: Norton, 1945.

Ferster, C. B. Positive reinforcement and behavioral deficits of autistic children. *Child Development,* 1961, 32, 437-456.

Fisher, S. Projective methodologies. In P. R. Farnsworth, O. McNemar & Q. McNemar (Eds.), *Annual review of psychology*, Vol. 18. Palo Alto, Calif.: Annual Reviews, 1967. Pp. 165-190.

Foulds, G. A. The reliability of psychiatric, and the validity of psychological, diagnoses. *Journal of Mental Science,* 1955, 101, 851-862.

Freeman, H. E. & Simmons, O. G. *The mental patient comes home.* New York: Wiley, 1963.

Freudenberg, R. & Robertson, J. Symptoms in relation to psychiatric diagnosis and treatment. *Archives of Neurology and Psychiatry,* 1956, 76, 14-22.

Fulkerson, S. D. & Barry, J. R. Methodology and research on the prognostic use of psychological tests. *Psychological Bulletin,* 1961, 58, 177-204.

Gamsky, N. R. & Farwell, G. F. Counselor verbal behavior as a function of client hostility. *Journal of Counseling Psychology,* 1966, 13, 184-190.

Garfield, S. L. The Rorschach test in clinical diagnosis. *Journal of Clinical Psychology,* 1947, 3, 375-381.

Garfield, S. L. The clinical method in personality assessment. In J. M. Wepman & R. W. Heine (Eds.), *Concepts of personality.* Chicago: Aldine, 1963. Pp. 474-502.

Gauron, E. F. & Dickinson, J. K. Diagnostic decision making in psychiatry. *Archives of General Psychiatry,* 1966, 14, 225-232.

Giedt, F. H. Comparison of visual, content and auditory cues in interviewing. *Journal of Consulting Psychology,* 1955, 19, 407-416.

Goldberg, L. R. & Werts, C. E. The reliability of clinicians' judgments: A multitrait-multimethod approach. *Journal of Consulting Psychology,* 1966, 30, 199-206.

Goldfarb, A. Reliability of diagnostic judgments by psychologists. *Journal of Clinical Psychology,* 1959, 15, 392-396.

Gordon, C. M. Some effects of information, situation and personality on decision making in a clinical setting. *Journal of Consulting Psychology,* 1966, 30, 219-224.

Gough, H. G., Wenk, E. A. & Rozynko, V. V. Parole outcome as predicted from the CPI, the MMPI and a base expectancy table. *Journal of Abnormal Psychology,* 1965, 70, 432-441.

Gravitz, H. L. & Handler, L. Effects of different modes of administration on the Bender Visual Motor Gestalt Test. *Journal of Consulting and Clinical Psychology,* 1968, 32, 276-279.

Grigg, A. E. Experience of clinicians and speech characteristics and statements of clients as variables in clinical judgments. *Journal of Consulting Psychology,* 1958, 22, 315-319.

Grosz, H. J. & Grossman, K. G. Clinician's response style: A source of variation and bias in clinical judgments. *Journal of Abnormal Psychology,* 1968, 73, 207-214.

Group for the Advancement of Psychiatry, Committee on Child Psychiatry. Psychopathological disorders in childhood: Theoretical considerations and a proposed classification. *Group for the Advancement of Psychiatry Reports,* 1966, 6(62), 173-343.

Hammer, E. F. Critique of Swensen's "empirical evaluations of human figure drawings." *Journal of Projective Techniques,* 1959, 23, 30-32.

Hathaway, S. R. Clinical intuition and inferential accuracy. *Journal of Personality,* 1956, 24, 223-250.

Heron, A. The effects of real-life motivation on questionnaire responses. *Journal of Applied Psychology,* 1956, 40, 65-68.

Hofstadter, R. *Social Darwinism in American thought.* Boston: Beacon Press, 1955.

Hollingshead, A. B. & Redlich, F. C. *Social class and mental illness.* New York: Wiley, 1958.

Holmes, G. *Introduction to clinical neurology.* Edinburgh: Livingstone, 1946.

Holt, R. R. & Luborsky, L. *Personality patterns of psychiatrists,* Vol. 1. *A Study of methods for selecting residents.* New York: Basic Books, 1958.

Holzberg, J. D. & Wexler, M. The validity of human form drawings as a measure of personality deviation. *Journal of Projective Techniques,* 1950, 14, 343-361.

Huff, F. W. Factors affecting agreement among clinicians. *Journal of General Psychology,* 1966, 75, 265-272.

Huff, F. W. & Friedman, H. A study of the effects on agreement among clinicians of redundant and new information, confidence and time available for assessments. *Journal of General Psychology,* 1967, 76, 49-57.

Hunt, R. C. & Appel, K. E. Prognosis in psychoses lying midway between schizophrenia and manic-depressive psychoses. *American Journal of Psychiatry,* 1936, 93, 313-339.

Hunt, W. A. The future of diagnostic testing in clinical psychology. *Journal of Clinical Psychology,* 1946, 2, 311-317.

Hunt, W. A., Wittson, C. L. & Hunt, E. A. A theoretical and practical analysis of the diagnostic process. In P. H. Hoch & J. Zubin (Eds.), *Current problems in psychiatric diagnosis.* New York: Grune & Stratton, 1953. Pp. 53-65.

Inglis, J. *The scientific study of abnormal behavior.* Chicago: Aldine, 1966.

Irwin, M., Tripodi, T. & Bieri, J. Affective stimulus value and cognitive complexity. *Journal of Personality and Social Psychology,* 1967, 5, 444-448.

Johnson, H. M. Some fallacies underlying the use of psychological tests. *Psychological Review,* 1928, 35, 328-337.

Johnston, R. & McNeal, B. F. Statistical vs. clinical prediction: Length of neuropsychiatric hospital stay. *Journal of Abnormal Psychology,* 1967, 72, 335-340.

Kaelbling, A. & Volpe, P. A. Constancy of psychiatric diagnoses in readmissions. *Comprehensive Psychiatry,* 1963, 4, 29-40.

Kanfer, F. H. & Saslow, G. Behavioral analysis: An alternative to diagnostic classification. *Archives of General Psychiatry,* 1965, 12, 529-538.

Kanfer, F. H. & Saslow, G. Behavioral diagnosis. In C. Franks (Ed.), *Assessment and status of the behavior therapies and associated developments.* New York: McGraw-Hill, in press.

Kantor, R. E. & Herron, W. G. *Reactive and process schizophrenia.* Palo Alto, Calif.: Science and Behavior Books, 1966.

Kelly, E. L. & Fiske, D. W. The prediction of success in the VA training program in clinical psychology. *American Psychologist,* 1950, 5, 395-406.

Kelly, E. L. & Fiske, D. W. *The prediction of performance in clinical psychology.* Ann Arbor: University of Michigan Press, 1951.

Kelly, G. A. *The psychology of personal constructs,* Vol. 1. New York: Norton, 1955.

Kessel, N. & Shepherd, M. Neurosis in hospital and general practice. *Journal of Mental Science,* 1962, 108, 159-166.

Klopfer, B., Ainsworth, M., Klopfer, G. & Holt, R. *Developments in Rorschach technique.* New York: World Book Co., 1954.

Kogan, L. S. Validity, reliability and related considerations. In A. W. Shyne (Ed.), *Use of judgments as data in social work research.* New York: National Association of Social Workers, 1959. Pp. 68-77.

Kostlan, A. A method for the empirical study of psychodiagnosis. *Journal of Consulting Psychology,* 1954, 18, 83-88.

Kreitman, N. The reliability of psychiatric diagnosis. *Journal of Mental Science,* 1961, 107, 876-886.

Kreitman, N., Sainsbury, P., Morrissey, J., Towers, J. & Scrivener, J. The reliability of psychiatric assessment: An analysis. *Journal of Mental Science,* 1961, 107, 887-908.

Kroger, R. O. Effects of implicit and explicit task cues upon personality test performance. *Journal of Consulting and Clinical Psychology,* 1968, 32, 498.

Lakin, M. & Lieberman, M. A. Diagnostic information and psychotherapists' conceptualization. *Journal of Clinical Psychology,* 1965, 21, 385-388.

Langfeldt, G. The diagnosis of schizophrenia. *American Journal of Psychiatry,* 1951, 108, 123-125.

Leifer, R. The psychiatrist and tests of criminal responsibility. *American Psychologist,* 1964, 19, 825-830.

Leventhal, H. Cognitive processes and interpersonal predictions. *Journal of Abnormal and Social Psychology,* 1957, 55, 176-180.

Lindemann, J. E., Fairweather, G. W., Stone, G. B., Smith, R. S. & London, I. T. The use of demographic characteristics in predicting length of neuro-psychiatric hospital stay. *Journal of Consulting Psychology,* 1959, 23, 85-90.

Linder, R. Diagnosis: Description or prescription. *Perceptual and Motor Skills,* 1965, 20, 1081-1092.

Lindsley, O. R. Operant conditioning methods applied to research in chronic schizophrenia. *Psychiatric Research Reports,* 1956, 5, 118-139.

Lindsley, O. R. Characteristics of the behavior of chronic psychotics as revealed by free-operant conditioning methods. *Diseases of the Nervous System, Monograph Supplement,* 1960, 21(2), 66-78.

Lindsley, O. R. Direct measurement and functional definition of vocal hallucinatory symptoms. *Journal of Nervous and Mental Diseases,* 1963, 136, 293-297.

Lindzey, G. Seer versus sign. *Journal of Experimental Research in Personality,* 1965, 1, 17-26.

Lipsher, D. H. Consistency of clinicians' judgments based on MMPI, Rorschach and TAT protocols. Paper presented at the Clinical Diagnosis Section, Annual Convention of the American Psychological Association, St. Louis, 1962.

Little, K. B. Problems in the validation of projective techniques. *Journal of Projective Techniques,* 1959, 23, 287-290.

Little, K. B. & Shneidman, E. S. Congruencies among interpretations of psychological test and anamnestic data. *Psychological Monographs,* 1959, 73, (6, Whole No. 476).

Lorge, I., Tuckman, J. & Dunn, M. B. Human figure drawings by younger and older adults. *American Psychologist,* 1954, 9, 420-421. (Abstract)

Lorr, M. & McNair, D. M. Methods relating to the evaluation of therapeutic outcome. In L. A. Gottschalk & A. H. Auerbach (Eds.), *Methods of research in psychotherapy.* New York: Appleton-Century-Crofts, 1966. Pp. 573-594.

Lowe, C. M. Prediction of posthospital work adjustment by the use of psychological tests. *Journal of Counseling Psychology,* 1967, 14, 248-252.

Luft, J. Implicit hypothesis and clinical predictions. *Journal of Abnormal and Social Psychology,* 1950, 45, 756-759.

Machover, K. *Personality projection in the drawing of the human figure.* Springfield, Ill.: Charles Thomas, 1949.

Mahrer, A. R. Psychodiagnostic preference by professional affiliation and length of experience. *Journal of Clinical Psychology,* 1962, 18, 14-18.

Martin, A. R. Emphasis on the healthy aspects of the patient in psychoanalysis. *American Journal of Psychoanalysis,* 1966, 26, 20.

Masling, J. The influence of situational and interpersonal variables in projective testing. *Psychological Bulletin,* 1960, 57, 65-85.

McDermott, J. F., Harrison, S. I., Schrager, J. & Wilson, P. Social class and mental illness: Observations of blue collar families. *American Journal of Orthopsychiatry,* 1965, 35, 500-508.

McPartland, T. S. & Richart, R. H. Social and clinical outcomes of psychiatric treatment. *Archives of General Psychiatry,* 1966, 14, 179-184.

Mechanic, D. Some factors in identifying and defining mental illness. *Mental Hygiene,* 1962, 46, 66-74.

Meehl, P. E. *Clinical versus statistical prediction.* Minneapolis: University of Minnesota Press, 1954.

Meehl, P. E. The cognitive activity of the clinician. *American Psychologist,* 1960, 15, 19-27.

Meehl, P. E. Seer over sign: The first good example. *Journal of Experimental Research in Personality,* 1965, 1, 27-32.

Mehlman, B. The reliability of psychiatric diagnoses. *Journal of Abnormal and Social Psychology,* 1952, 47, 577-578.

Michael, J. C. & Buhler, C. Experiences with personality testing in a neuropsychiatric department of a public general hospital. *Diseases of the Nervous System,* 1945, 6, 205-211.

Miller, G. A. The magical number seven, plus-or-minus two: Some limits on our capacity for processing information. *Psychological Review,* 1956, 63, 81-97.

Miller, H. & Bieri, J. An informational analysis of clinical judgment. *Journal of Abnormal and Social Psychology,* 1963, 67, 317-325.

Miller, R. R. An experimental study of the observational process in casework. *Social Work,* 1958, 3(2), 96-102.

Mills, D. H. & Abeles, N. Counselor needs for affiliation and nurturance as related to liking for clients and counseling process. *Journal of Counseling Psychology,* 1965, 12, 353-358.

Mintz, J. Survey of student therapists' attitudes toward psychodiagnostic reports. *Journal of Consulting and Clinical Psychology,* 1968, 32, 500.

Mogar, R. E. Anxiety indices in human figure drawings: A replication and extension. *Journal of Consulting Psychology,* 1962, 26, 108.

Moos, R. H. Situational analysis of a therapeutic community milieu. *Journal of Abnormal Psychology,* 1968, 73, 49-61.

Moos, R. H. & Clemes, S. R. Multivariate study of the patient-therapist system. *Journal of Consulting Psychology,* 1967, 31, 119-130.

Osgood, C., Suci, G. & Tannenbaum, P. *The measurement of meaning.* Urbana: University of Illinois Press, 1957.

Parker, C. As a clinician thinks. *Journal of Counseling Psychology,* 1958, 5, 253-262.

Parsons, O. A. & Stewart, K. D. Effects of supportive versus disinterested interviews on perceptual-motor performance in brain-damaged and neurotic patients. *Journal of Consulting Psychology,* 1966, 30, 260-266.

Pasamanick, B., Roberts, D. W., Lemkau, P. W. & Krueger, D. B. A survey of mental disease in an urban population: Prevalence by race and income. In F. Riessman, J. Cohen & A. Pearl (Eds.), *Mental health of the poor.* New York: Free Press, 1964. Pp. 39-48.

Patrick, J. H., Overall, J. E. & Tupin, J. P. Multiple discriminant analysis of clinical diagnostic groups. In American Psychological Association, *Proceedings of the 76th Annual Convention of the APA.* Washington, D.C.: American Psychological Association, 1968. Pp. 465-466.

Payne, R. W. Diagnostic and personality testing in clinical psychology. *American Journal of Psychiatry,* 1958, 115, 25-29.

Peterson, D. R. Scope and generality of verbally defined personality factors. *Psychological Review,* 1965, 72, 48-59.

Plotnick, H. L. The relation between selected personality characteristics of social work students and accuracy in predicting behavior of clients. Unpublished doctoral dissertation, Columbia University School of Social Work, 1961.

Pope, B. & Scott, W. H. *Psychological diagnosis in clinical practice.* New York: Oxford University Press, 1967.

Raines, G. N. & Rohmer, J. H. The operational matrix of psychiatric practice, I: Consistency and variability in interview impressions of different psychiatrists. *American Journal of Psychiatry,* 1955, 111, 721-733.

Rapaport, D. & Schafer, R. *Manual of diagnostic testing, II. Diagnostic testing of personality and ideational content.* New York: Joshiah Macy Jr. Foundation, 1946.

Rice, V. Social class as a dimension in casework judgments. *Smith College Studies in Social Work,* 1963, 34, 30-48.

Rotter, J. B. *Social learning and clinical psychology.* New York: Prentice-Hall, 1954.

Rotter, J. B. Can the clinician learn from experience? *Journal of Consulting Psychology,* 1967, 31, 12-15.

Rubin, H. The Minnesota Multiphasic Personality Inventory as a diagnostic aid in a veterans hospital. *Journal of Consulting Psychology,* 1948, 12, 251-254.

Rumke, H. C. Contradictions in the concepts of schizophrenia. *Comprehensive Psychiatry,* 1960, 1, 331-337.

Sarbin, T. R. On the futility of the proposition that some people be labeled "mentally ill." *Journal of Consulting Psychology,* 1967, 31, 447-453.

Sarbin, T. R., Taft, R. & Bailey, D. E. *Clinical inference and cognitive theory.* New York: Holt, Rinehart & Winston, 1960.

Sawyer, J. Measurement and prediction, clinical and statistical. *Psychological Bulletin,* 1966, 66, 178-200.

Scarbrough, H. E. The nature of the dialogue with the obsessive compulsive. *Psychotherapy: Theory, Research and Practice,* 1966, 3, 33-35.

Scheff, T. Decision rules, types of errors, and their consequences in medical diagnosis. *Behavioral Science,* 1963, 8, 97-107.

Schmidt, H. O. & Fonda, C. P. The reliability of psychiatric diagnosis: A new look. *Journal of American Sociology,* 1956, 52, 262-267.

Schuessler, K. F. & Cressey, D. B. Personality characteristics of criminals. *American Journal of Sociology,* 1950, 55, 476-484.

Schwartz, M. L. Validity and reliability in clinical judgments of C-V-S protocols as a function of amount of information and diagnostic category. *Psychological Reports,* 1967, 20, 767-774.

Shneidman, E. S. Suggestions for delineation of validity studies. *Journal of Projective Techniques,* 1959, 23, 259-262.

Sines, L. K. An experimental-investigation of the relative contribution to clinical diagnosis and personality description of various kinds of pertinent data. Unpublished doctoral dissertation, University of Minnesota, 1957.

Sines, L. K. The relative contribution of four kinds of data to accuracy in personality assessment. *Journal of Consulting Psychology,* 1959, 23, 483-492.

Skolnick, A. Motivational imagery and behavior over twenty years. *Journal of Consulting Psychology,* 1966, 30, 463-478.

Small, J. G., Saunders, J. E., Small, I. F. & Morton, P. M. Awareness of illness as related to psychiatric diagnosis: Clinical course and treatment setting. *American Journal of Psychotherapy,* 1967, 21, 220-229.

Smith, J. & Lanyon, R. I. Prediction of juvenile probation violators. *Journal of Consulting and Clinical Psychology,* 1968, 32, 54-58.

Soskin, W. F. Bias in postdiction from projective tests. *Journal of Abnormal and Social Psychology,* 1954, 49, 65-74.

Soskin, W. F. Influence of 4 types of data on diagnostic conceptualization in psychological testing. *Journal of Abnormal and Social Psychology,* 1959, 58, 69-78.

Street, D., Vinter, R. D. & Perrow, C. *Organization for treatment.* New York: Free Press, 1966.

Stuart, R. B. Promise and paradox in socioeconomic status conceptions. *Smith College Studies in Social Work,* 1965, 35, 110-124.

Stuart, R. B. Association between verbal aspects of assessment and successful and unsuccessful casework treatment. Unpublished manuscript, University of Michigan, 1968.

Sundberg, N. D. The practice of psychological testing in clinical services in the United States. *American Psychologist,* 1961, 16, 79-83.

Swensen, C. H. Empirical evaluations of human figure drawings. *Psychological Bulletin,* 1957, 54, 431-466.

Szasz, T. The myth of mental illness. *American Psychologist,* 1960, 15, 113-118.

Taft, R. The ability to judge people. *Psychological Bulletin,* 1955, 52, 1-28.

Thorne, F. C. *Clinical judgment: A study of clinical errors.* Brandon, Vt.: Journal of Clinical Psychology, 1961.

Tripodi, T. Cognitive complexity and the perception of conflict: A partial replication. *Perceptual and Motor Skills,* 1967, 25, 543-544.

Tripodi, T. & Bieri, J. Information transmission in clinical judgments as a function of stimulus dimensionality and cognitive complexity. *Journal of Personality,* 1964, 32, 119-137.

Tripodi, T. & Bieri, J. Cognitive complexity, perceived conflict, and certainty. *Journal of Personality,* 1966, 34, 144-153.

Tripodi, T. & Miller, H. The clinical judgment process: A review of the literature. *Social Work,* 1966, 11(3), 63-69.

Turner, R. & Tripodi, T. Cognitive complexity as a function of type of stimulus objects judged and affective stimulus value. *Journal of Consulting and Clinical Psychology,* 1968, 32, 182-185.

Turner, R. J. & Cumming, J. Theoretical malaise and community mental health. In E. L. Cowen, E. A. Gardner & M. Zax (Eds.), *Emergent approaches to mental health problems.* New York: Appleton-Century-Crofts, 1967. Pp. 40-62.

Waldo, G. P. & Dinitz, S. Personality attributes of the criminal: An analysis of research studies, 1950-65. *Journal of Research in Crime and Delinquency,* 1967, 4, 185-202.

Wallon, E. J. A study of criteria used to differentiate the human-figure drawings of normals, neurotics and psychotics. Unpublished doctoral dissertation, Purdue University, 1959.

Wanderer, Z. W. The validity of diagnostic judgments based on "blind" Machover figure drawings. Unpublished doctoral dissertation, Columbia University, 1964.

Wanderer, Z. W. The validity of diagnostic judgments based on "blind" Machover figure drawings. *Dissertation Abstracts,* 1966, 26, 67-68.

Watson, C. Relationship of distortion to DAP diagnostic accuracy among psychologists at three levels of sophistication. *Journal of Consulting Psychology,* 1967, 31, 142-146.

Watson, R. I. Psychology: A prescriptive science. *American Psychologist,* 1967, 22, 435-443.

Weiss, J. H. The effect of professional training, amount of information, and correctness of information on accuracy of prediction. Unpublished doctoral dissertation, State University of Iowa, 1962.

Weiss, J. H. Effect of professional training and amount and accuracy of information on behavioral prediction. *Journal of Consulting Psychology,* 1963, 27, 257-262.

Wilcox, R. & Krasnoff, A. Influence of test-taking attitudes on personality inventory scores. *Journal of Consulting Psychology,* 1967, 37, 188-194.

Wirt, R. D. & Briggs, P. F. Personality and environmental factors in the development of delinquency. *Psychological Monographs,* 1959, 73(15, Whole No. 485).

Wittenborn, J. R. The behavioral symptoms for certain organic psychoses. *Journal of Consulting Psychology,* 1952, 16, 104-106.

Wittenborn, J. R. & Bailey, C. The symptoms of involutional psychosis. *Journal of Consulting Psychology,* 1952, 16, 13-17.

Wittenborn, J., Holzberg, J. & Simon, B. Symptom correlates for descriptive diagnosis. *Genetic Psychology Monographs,* 1953, 47, 237-301.

Wittenborn, J. R. & Weiss, W. Patients diagnosed manic depressive psychosis—manic state. *Journal of Consulting Psychology,* 1952, 16, 193-198.

Zigler, E. & Butterfield, E. C. Motivational aspects of change in IQ test performance of culturally deprived nursery school children. *Child Development,* 1968, 39, 1-15.

Zigler, E. & Phillips, L. Psychiatric diagnosis and symptomatology. *Journal of Abnormal and Social Psychology,* 1961, 63, 69-75. (a)

Zigler, E. & Phillips, L. Psychiatric diagnosis: A critique. *Journal of Abnormal and Social Psychology,* 1961, 3, 607-618. (b)

5
Iatrogenic Effects
of Dispositional Labels

In Chapter 4 it was argued that dispositional labels which are the product of mental status examination or psychological testing may be both unreliable and invalid. The major danger inherent in low reliability is arbitrariness in the use of categories, while the major danger inherent in low validity is formulation of unproductive treatment decisions. Therefore the use of an unreliable and invalid clinical vocabulary carries with it the risk of offering treatment which is not helpful and is potentially harmful. This chapter will consider some of the potential dangers in using the dispositional diagnostic system in light of its limitations. If dispositional diagnosis were reasonably reliable or likely to lead to meaningful treatment decisions, the risks which will be noted in this chapter might be worth taking. In light of the evidence which has already been reviewed, however, it would seem that the risks in the use of such labels could well outweigh the potential rewards in their use.

Semantics and Negative Labels

When an individual is given a dispositional diagnosis, he receives a negative label owing to the pathological character of the clinical nosology (Ellis, 1967; Maslow, 1948; Sarbin, 1967). It is generally agreed (Jahoda, 1958; Scott, 1961) that there is no commonly acceptable description of a "healthy personality," and neither of the two most frequently used clinical nosologies (American Psychiatric Association, 1952; Group for the Advancement of Psychiatry, 1966) includes more than passing reference to categories of healthy functioning relative to the vast array of references to unhealthy functioning. Therefore, a diagnostic label is clearly a negative label, and one which is drawn without clear reference to a conception of positive functioning.

Once a negative label has been applied, there is a clear and present danger that the person so identified will be the victim of additional negative inference solely on the basis of his having been designated as a deviant, without reference either to the behavior which culminated in his having been labeled or to any subsequent actions on his part. The evidence that supports this view is rather convincing. For example, it has been shown that negative adjectives exert a disproportionate influence upon the nouns with which they are associated. Osgood, Suci and Tannenbaum (1957, pp. 275-284) found that when "treacherous" is associated with "nurse" the semantic differential value of nurse falls sharply, while when "sincere" is associated with "prostitute" the prostitute does not undergo a comparable rise in valuation. Research by Stuart (1968a) has provided additional tentative support for this hypothesis. It has been shown, for example, that the semantic differential rating given to two positive adjectives paired with one negative adjective differs only very slightly from that given to the negative adjective alone. This relationship is seen to hold despite the order of presentation, while a recency effect is evident when three adjectives of like sign but differing polarity are presented.

Several studies have gone further than merely identifying the general semantic effect of negative labels. These studies have been concerned with what inferences their subjects draw from commonly used labels relevant to "mental illness" (Giovannoni & Ullmann, 1963; Manis, Houts & Blake, 1963). For example, one study (Crumpton, Weinstein, Acker & Annis, 1967) demonstrated that from 51 to 82 per cent of respondents thought that any person who was identified as a "mental patient" must be "excitable," "foolish," "unsuccessful," "unusual," "slow," "untimely," "passive," "cruel," "weak," "curved" and "ugly." Therefore it can be concluded that merely making public that an individual has been assigned to a deviance category exposes him to the very general negative judgments of others, judgments which go far beyond what may have been intended when the label was first used.

Effect of Negative Labels upon the Patient

When a patient or members of his family receive a diagnosis, an intense emotional response is likely to result. One reaction might be relief stemming from the fact that at least the severe distress has a label. But at the same time

> . . .it introduces a new kind of fear, fear not of the actual condition as it exists but of the condition which is implied— usually incorrectly—by the exotic name [Menninger, 1963, p. 44].

How many patients, or how many professionals for that matter, realize that when a diagnostic label is used, it usually refers to only a very small proportion of an individual's complex repertoire of behaviors? For example, how many people realize that "neurotics" brush their teeth, say "good morning" and walk to work in much the same manner as the rest of us? To the extent that this important reality is overlooked, the mere ascription of a label can have very fear-arousing effects.

A second profound change was eloquently described by Erik Erikson (1964) in the following terms:

> [When the patient is given a diagnosis,] 'insult is added to injury' in that the uprooted one, already considered expendable or abnormal by his previous group affiliations, finds himself categorized and judged by those who were expected to show him the way through a meaningful moratorium. Many a man acquires the irreversible identity of being a lifelong patient

and client not on the basis of what he 'is,' but on the basis
of what is first done about him [p. 97].

Thus when the patient undergoes the social ritual of being
labeled as a diagnostic entity, he is likely to think of himself
in clinical terms, lower his expectations for his own behavior
and demand more of others. It can also be hypothesized that
the availability of a diagnostic label creates the opportunity
for negative self-stimulation by the patient leading to emission of deviant behaviors consistent with that label.

Effect of Negative Labels upon Social and Professional Interaction

Viewed in the abstract, the personal effects of dispositional
diagnostic labeling might not be considered too serious and
in fact might even be regarded by some as having therapeutic value to the extent that they may shock the patient
into altered behavior. Unfortunately, however, it has been
shown that the negative labeling of an individual leads others
to respond to him negatively. One recent investigation
(Farina, Holland & Ring, 1966) offered college students an
opportunity to shock an experimental confederate in a
training exercise. It was found that the amount of shock
administered varied as a function of the amount of stigma
contained in background descriptions of the confederates.
One can easily speculate that once family members are
apprised that a troublesome person in their midst has been
diagnosed as mentally ill, the same set of negative reactions
may ensue.

The labeling process may also exert a strong effect upon
therapist-patient interaction. In Chapter 3 it was pointed out
that one of the weaknesses in psychoanalytic psychotherapy,
particularly as it draws upon dream interpretation, may be
the "seeding" and reinforcement of dream content. A therapist equipped with a dispositional diagnosis may be equally
vulnerable to the tendency to seed pathology-relevant
behaviors.

That therapists verbally influence their patients has been virtually unchallenged since the work of numerous investigators such as Greenspoon (1955), Verplanck (1955), Krasner (1958) and Salzinger (1959). It is hypothesized that therapists accelerate certain classes of patient responses by encouraging and attending to them while decelerating other classes of responses by criticizing or ignoring them (Quay, 1959; Staats, Staats, Heard & Finley, 1962). Furthermore, it can be postulated that this interaction is inevitable, as even Carl Rogers has been shown to influence his patients in this manner (Truax, 1966). When the therapist has promulgated a diagnosis and seeks to understand his patient in its terms, it is highly probable that his differential responses will be contingent upon the patient's emission of verbal responses that are congruent with this conception. Since this conception is almost invariably negative, owing to the character of clinical nosology, it can be seen that the very existence of a diagnosis may influence the therapist-patient interaction in an antitherapeutic direction.

Negative Labeling and Social Opportunity

Just as negative labels can materially affect the character of the patient's interaction with his family and therapist, so too can the effects of labels be seen in the patient's dealings with the larger social community. One of the most ingenious studies of this effect was the work of Schwartz and Skolnick (1962), who sent letters to employers asking whether they would consider hiring a man who (a) had a court record, (b) had been acquitted of a charge, or (c) had been acquitted of an offense with an apologetic letter from the judge attached to the inquiry. The predictable result was that there was little difference in the prospective employer's unwillingness to hire the applicant even if he had been acquitted. A study by Stuart (1968b) also supports this finding insofar as less than .25 scale point separates negative ratings of "arrested," "convicted," or "in prison," while "acquitted" is only .41 (SD = 1.99) above the average of the first three. Therefore potential employers may close opportunities to job applicants who bear labels even loosely related to deviance.

The operation of deviance labels in work-related programs in mental hospitals is another area in which diagnosed patients can be shown to suffer. Brink, Oetting and Cole (1967) followed the careers of 249 patients from the Fort Logan Mental Health Center. One hundred seventy-two of the patients were placed in work settings, 105 of whom had successful placements. Two findings of this research are of particular note. First, it was found that clinical diagnosis—i.e., psychosis, neurosis and personality disorder—was not associated with success in work placement. Second, it was found that 38 per cent of the psychotics were not placed, in contrast to 24 per cent of the neurotics and 19 per cent of the personality disorders. If the diagnoses had been shown to be relevant to the outcome of placement, then they might have had a degree of validity. In view of the results, however, the authors conclude:

> One could speculate that the project staff have developed a 'set' or a bias in their typical pattern of decision making in regard to release of patients from psychiatric hospitals. That is, after a patient has once received the label of psychotic or schizophrenic, it is not unrealistic to consider the possibility that professional people then tend to judge this patient in terms of the label that is attached to him rather than in terms of his actual overt behavior [Brink, Oetting & Cole, 1967, p. 38].

When diagnosis failed to emerge as an effective predictor of which patients were successfully placed, other possibilities were sought. One of the seven factors which were shown to be effective was "insight into their illness [Brink, Oetting & Cole, 1967, p. 40]." Insight, in turn, can be translated into "expressing the same ideas about illness as were expressed by the therapist," and it can be argued that this expressed agreement with the labels which are used by the therapist may be more influential in determining patient career than other more important aspects of his functioning.

The decision to hospitalize patients accused of criminal acts has also been shown to be under the strong influence of dispositional diagnosis, usually to the patient's detriment (Jeffery, 1964; Leifer, 1964; Stuart, 1969; Szasz, 1961). Furthermore, it has been shown that most inmates who received negative diagnoses also received poor prognoses (Sarri, 1962). These negative prognostic statements must undoubtedly influence the behavior of the staff towards the inmate and ultimately must affect the alternatives that are made available to the patient.

The effect of both positive and negative labeling has been clearly identified in the careers of school children. Rosenthal and his associates (Anderson & Rosenthal, 1968; Conn, Edwards, Rosenthal & Crowne, 1968; Rosenthal, 1966) have engaged in a series of studies which demonstrate the complex interrelationship between teacher expectation and student performance. One of the more fully reported studies (Rosenthal & Jacobson, 1968) contained a very vivid demonstration of the power of teacher expectation in their study of "Oak School." All children in three classes at each of six grade levels were administered a nonverbal test of intelligence. The teachers of a randomly selected group of one fifth of the children were told that these particular children revealed themselves to be "academic bloomers" and that great academic strides could be expected during the ensuing year. The following June, the same tests were readministered and the results were compared with the earlier assessment. It was found that while the children in the control group (not identified as "bloomers") "gained well in IQ, 19 percent gaining over twenty or more total IQ points [p. 176]," 47 percent of the "special" children gained 20 or more total IQ points. The inescapable conclusion of this study is that teacher expectation may be as important an influence upon student performance as any other single factor, including the student's endowment and preschool experience.

Just as labeling can have a positive effect, so too can it have a distinctly negative effect. For example, it has been suggested that schools have well-developed formal and informal mechanisms for the diffusion of negative reports about students, so that reports of minor disturbances which arise in one classroom are quickly passed along to all members of the faculty and the student body as well (Schafer & Polk, 1967, pp. 251-253). The effect of this diffusion can be seen both cross-sectionally, in a general reduction in acceptance of the labeled child's behavior, and longitudinally, in the closing of subsequent educational alternatives to children who are identified as "red tag" cases (Cowen, Zax, Izzo & Trost, 1966).

As another example of the effect of identifying children as atypical, Cicourel and Kitsuse (1963) showed that students may be assigned to different programs within the same school on the basis of testing and that, independent of intelligence or performance, the children assigned to "academic" classes uniformly receive higher grades than students in classes euphemistically identified as "opportunity" programs. The student's grade level, in turn, substantially influences his access to further training, so that a vicious cycle is instituted by the apparently innocent act of labeling.

A second study came to an even more distressing conclusion. While it is commonly asserted that students who are "malperformers" or "underachievers" in school are unmotivated, this study showed that:

> more often than not students in trouble differ little if any from nondeviants in the extent to which they are concerned about succeeding in school as well as in later life [Schafer, 1967, p. 56]

In another study (Stuart, 1968a), the effects of labeling have been correlated with prognosis and outcome in psychotherapy. One hundred twenty-seven experienced, professional social workers were each asked to write case vignettes containing the following data about one currently open and one closed case: presenting problem, a brief description of the patient, a brief description of the treatment used, and either a brief statement of prognosis (for the current cases) or a brief evaluation of outcome (for the closed cases). The first finding was a statistically significant association between the number of negative trait adjectives contained in the descriptions of the patient and the ratings of prognosis or outcome. In order to explore the possibility that this association might be a function of actual limitations in the patients' functioning, a second test was performed. A second group of social workers was asked to rate the severity and prognosis for each of the presenting problems contained in the original vignettes. It was found that these ratings correlated neither with the original worker's number of trait references nor with the prognosis or outcome. Therefore, it was concluded that negative bias in the worker, as reflected in the number of negative trait references used in describing the client, is a more potent predictor of prognosis and outcome than is presenting complaint. Finally, it was shown that the probability that the client would be referred elsewhere for treatment was directly proportional to the number of negative adjectives used to describe the client.

In addition to negatively biasing the patient's opportunities with respect to occupational, academic and therapeutic alternatives, labeling may also have a profoundly negative influence upon his civil rights (NASW Opposes, 1967). In a particularly bad situation, the American Civil Liberties Union entered complaints in behalf of 800 "defective delinquents" who were sentenced to indefinite terms in the Dallas, Pennsylvania, training school. The process of commitment to the institution was summarized by ACLU in the following terms:

> He need never have been accused—much less convicted with due process—of a criminal act; 'delinquency' is enough. He may well have been found delinquent at a five-minute hearing at which he did not know the specific charges against him, at which hearsay evidence was admitted, at which no cross-examination was allowed, and at which he could not procure witnesses. Almost certainly he

was not represented by a lawyer, and he may have been told by the probation staff that he didn't need one. This boy, under the Defective Delinquent Act, can spend his life in prison on the grounds that he is *'defective'* and has 'criminal tendencies' [Coxe, 1966, p. 2, italics mine].

Dispositional Labels and Treatment Planning

In principle, the diagnostic process should result in an identification of the principal problems faced by a patient and should lead to the planning of treatment which, ideally, culminates in alleviation of the distress. In practice, unfortunately, the dispositional diagnosis may be used for administrative decision-making (Caveny, Wittson, Hunt & Herrmann, 1955), may serve to foreclose alternative social opportunities and may also obviate or obstruct treatment.

Bahn and Norman (1959) studied the patients of 499 mental health clinics. Of each ten patients for whom service was terminated, two received partial service such as an intake interview and referral elsewhere (averaging one interview contact for adults and two interview contacts for children), three received both diagnosis and treatment (averaging eight interview contacts for adults and seventeen interview contacts for children) and five received diagnosis but no treatment (averaging two interview contacts for adults and four interview contacts for children). In short, approximately half of all mental health clinic patients receive no treatment beyond diagnosis. Some of these may have been considered to be unneedful of treatment, although many of the persons in this group are likely to have been screened out prior to scheduling for diagnosis. Many of these people, on the other hand, were probably excluded from subsequent treatment on the basis of diagnostic considerations. Thus, professional labeling can indeed serve to foreclose therapeutic alternatives for some prospective patients.

In addition, dispositional labels may obstruct treatment because of their metaphoric character. Virtually all of the classes of clinical nosology are premised upon metaphoric references to some domain outside of psychology. Adams (1964) has made a list of five classes of such metaphors:

(1)   Pseudomedical analogies—e.g., mental illness
(2)   Pseudophysical analogies—e.g., mechanism, adjustment
(3)   Pseudobiological analogies—e.g., homeostasis
(4)   Pseudoelectronic analogies—e.g., input-output
(5)   Pseudogenitourinary and pseudogastrointestinal analogies—
      e.g,, urethral character and anal-expulsive expression.

As Sarbin (1967, 1968) has indicated, these analogies quickly lose their metaphoric character. Statements which originate as "as if" propositions assume the character of statements of fact and themselves become the basis of inference to still higher order abstractions. There is a logical flaw in such reasoning which is obvious: A term which is introduced as a predicate is used *in place of* the noun which it was to have elaborated.

Two illustrations of faulty treatment decisions based upon metaphoric confusion will suffice to illustrate its effect. In the first instance, it has been noted that children who may not perform well in school behave "as if" they had motivational problems. From that time onward, the child is treated as though he were in fact unmotivated.

> . . .we have continually observed that teachers, disciplinarians, and others frequently proceed on the false assumption that low commitment lies at the base of the problem and thus gear their responses toward increasing motivation and concern about success, rather than toward developing skills [Schafer, 1967, p. 56].

Thus the child who is in need of academic training is denied such training in deference to emphasis upon a dispositional problem. When he is denied relevant academic instruction, he falls further behind grade expectation, is classed as more deviant and undergoes still more academic disruption.

In the second instance, it has been observed that children suffering from childhood autism "react so inadequately to noises and voices that they have often been considered as deaf... They try to shut out all stimuli from the external world in order to remain more comfortable in their own world [Finch, 1960, p. 182]." This statement contains three elements: (a) it contains an observation (couched in evaluative terms —"inadequately"—rather than in descriptive language) that children do not emit expected responses to (some? all?) sounds; (b) it contains an implied premise that this low responsivity can be construed as withdrawal; and (c) it concludes that this responding is purposive and is designed to ensure the child's comfort (see also Skinner, 1967). There are two points that bear emphasis. First, it is vital to note that the conclusion which should properly be stated as propositional—it *appears as if* the children try to shut out stimuli..."—is stated declaratively instead. It is presented *as if* it were fact. Second, it is noteworthy that there is no means of testing whether or not children "try" to do anything "in order to remain more comfortable." These are mentalistic notions which imply internal antecedent stimuli, internal and external responses and internal consequences, and none of these internal events can be observed.

If a therapeutic program were based upon this metaphor, it might take the form of providing a low-key environment which seeks not to intrude upon the child's "consciousness," preferring instead to respond to his efforts to overcome his own "withdrawal." The staff in such an environment would talk softly and walk quietly in an effort not to disturb the autistic child's sensibilities. If this were the case, the environment might be exactly contrary to the needs of the child.

In an investigation which requires replication before its results can be fully accepted, Metz (1967) has found that "autistic children prefer, and will act to maintain, higher levels of auditory stimulation, as compared with successful and schizophrenic children [p. 534]." Using a conjugate schedule of reinforcement, children were given an opportunity to respond differentially in order to maintain high- or low-volume narration, among other auditory inputs, and it was found that autistic children consistently worked to maintain high volume. If the results of this study are replicated, then treatment programs for autistic children should contain consistent efforts to provide high-volume auditory stimulation for them in order to deal with what may be either a functional hearing loss or a simple preference for loud sounds. Providing a quiet environment, on the other hand, might well have the very harmful effect of reducing the availability of stimuli necessary for acceptable responses to social demands.

If labeling does not suggest a totally erroneous therapeutic course, it may suggest leads which are essentially irrelevant for the patient. Again it should be recalled that dispositional diagnosis is heavily pathology-oriented. When treatment is oriented to symptom removal, it may be oriented to changing behavior which is not central to the patient's maintaining himself in a socially acceptable manner in the community. For example, it has been shown that parents' complaints included only 17 per cent of the symptoms discovered in the diagnostic evaluations of children in one clinic (Novick, Rosenfeld, Bloch & Dawson, 1966). The clinic, then, went considerably beyond the pathological concern of the parents. Then, too, it has been shown that members of different environments respond differentially to different forms of problematic behavior in patients occupying differing roles and statuses (Dinitz, Lefton, Angrist & Pasamanick, 1961; Freeman & Simmons, 1963). Such treatment may be irrelevant or even harmful to the extent that it seeks "to change the feelings, anxieties and moods (or at least the patient's report about them) rather than to investigate the life conditions, interpersonal reactions and environmental factors which produce and maintain these habitual response patterns [Kanfer & Saslow, in press]."

Summary

The evidence which has been presented in this chapter supports the notion that mere assignment of a diagnostic label to a patient may prejudice his therapeutic experience and/or the course of the response which he receives from the organized social community. If the labels were shown to have high reliability and validity, exposure to this "secondary deviance" (deviance imposed by social institutions and of which the individual is essentially innocent) might be warranted. But dispositional diagnostic labels do not have this scientific character. Rotter (1960, p. 407) has referred to their propaganda value as opposed to their informational value, while Sarbin (1967) has argued that the labels are "vacuous, save as an epithet of pejoration [because they are of little scientific value because of their] reliance on an out-worn mentalistic concept—the ghost in the machine. . . [p. 453]." Menninger (1963) went even further, referring to dispositional labeling as "pejorative name calling [p. 47]," which he regarded as a further affliction visited upon the patient which adds to his distress.

In view of this recognition of the vicious cycle of distress → diagnosis → greater distress, one may wonder why self-corrective action has not led to amelioration of an unacceptable situation. A sample of the reasoning process that leads to a continued acceptance of this unacceptable practice is seen in a recent article by Ellis (1967). After noting several objections to dispositional labeling, Ellis seemingly overlooks their power and concludes that dispositional assessment procedures may be retained so long as they are utilized judiciously. But Ellis' reasoning is fraught with paradoxes. For example, his early statement that: "A person who is set apart as being emotionally aberrant may become so resentful of this kind of segregation that he may refuse to acknowledge his 'persecutors" efforts to help him and may get into hostile encounters with them and others that only serve to increase his living handicaps [p. 439]" is apparently forgotten when he later states: "Accepting the fact that he is emotionally sick may give an individual an incentive to improve his lot [p. 440]." For Ellis's patients, it is apparently possible to reject and accept assessment just as it is possible for Ellis to condemn yet condone a negative labeling practice. It is tragic that the same type of paradoxical thinking leads to the perpetuation of programs of psychiatric hospitalization and psychotherapy. These problems can be overcome only when the mental health ideology is purged of self-serving (Stuart, 1969) paradoxes and when it is instead based upon prudent use of the outcomes of empirical research.

In the following chapter, the various problems of dispositional diagnosis will be illustrated through presentation of the facts of one case. It will be shown that the dispositional diagnosis contributed to the failure of treatment in general and to deterioration of the patient's functioning in specific areas. This case will illustrate, then, the role played by dispositional diagnosis in iatrogenic illness.

References

Adams, H. "Mental illness" or interpersonal behavior? *American Psychologist,* 1964, 19, 191-197.

American Psychiatric Association. *Diagnostic and statistical manual of mental disorders.* Washington, D.C.: American Psychiatric Association, 1952.

Anderson, D. F. & Rosenthal, R. Some effects of interpersonal expectancy and social interaction on institutionalized retarded children. In American Psychological Association, *Proceedings of the 76th annual convention of the APA.* Washington, D.C.: American Psychological Association, 1968. Pp. 479-480.

Bahn, A. K. & Norman, V. B. First national report of patients in mental health clinics. *Public Health Reports,* 1959, 74, 943-956.

Brink, R. W., Oetting, E. R. & Cole, C. W. Technical research report number X: Predicting post-hospital outcome of psychiatric patients. Unpublished paper, Mental Health and Manpower Project, Colorado State University, 1967.

Caveny, E. L., Wittson, C. L., Hunt, W. A. & Herrmann, R. S. Psychiatric diagnosis: Its nature and function. *Journal of Nervous and Mental Diseases,* 1955, 121, 367-373.

Cicourel, A. V. & Kitsuse, J. I. *The educational decision makers.* Indianapolis: Bobbs Merrill, 1963.

Conn, L., Edwards, E., Rosenthal, R. & Crowne, D. Perception of emotion and response to teachers' expectancy by elementary school children. *Psychological Reports,* 1968, 22, 27-34.

Cowen, E. L., Zax, M., Izzo, L. D. & Trost, M. A. Prevention of emotional disorders in the school setting. *Journal of Consulting Psychology,* 1966, 30, 381-387.

Coxe, S. The great Dallas jailbreak. *Civil Liberties,* December 1966, 242. P. 2.

Crumpton, E., Weinstein, A. D., Acker, C. W. & Annis, A. P. How patients and normals see the mental patient. *Journal of Clinical Psychology,* 1967, 23, 46-49.

Dinitz, S., Lefton, M., Angrist, S. & Pasamanick, B. Psychiatric and social attributes as predictors of case outcome in mental hospitalization. *Social Problems,* 1961, 8, 322-328.

Ellis, A. Should some people be labeled mentally ill? *Journal of Consulting Psychology,* 1967, 31, 435-446.

Erikson, E. H. Identity and uprootedness in our time. In E. H. Erikson (Ed.), *Identity and responsibility.* New York: Norton, 1964. Pp. 81-109.

Farina, A., Holland, C. H. & Ring, K. Role of stigma and set in interpersonal interaction. *Journal of Abnormal Psychology,* 1966, 71, 421-428.

Finch, S. M. *Fundamentals of child psychiatry.* New York: Norton, 1960.

Freeman, H. E. & Simmons, O. G. *The mental patient comes home.* New York: Wiley, 1963.

Giovannoni, J. M. & Ullmann, L. P. Conceptions of mental health held by psychiatric patients. *Journal of Clinical Psychology,* 1963, 19, 398-400.

Greenspoon, J. The reinforcing effect of two spoken sounds on the frequency of two responses. *American Journal of Psychology,* 1955, 68, 409-416.

Group for the Advancement of Psychiatry, Committee on Child Psychiatry. Psychopathological disorders in childhood: Theoretical considerations and a proposed classification. *Group for the Advancement of Psychiatry Reports,* 1966, 6(62), 173-343.

Jahoda, M. *Current concepts of positive mental health.* New York: Basic Books, 1958.

Jeffery, R. The psychologist as an expert witness on the issue of insanity. *American Psychologist,* 1964, 19, 838-843.

Kanfer, F. H. & Saslow, G. Behavioral diagnosis. In C. Franks (Ed.), *Assessment and status of the behavior therapies and associated developments.* New York: McGraw-Hill, in press.

Krasner, L. Studies of the conditioning of verbal behavior. *Psychological Bulletin,* 1958, 55, 148-170.

Leifer, R. The psychiatrist and tests of criminal responsibility. *American Psychologist,* 1964, 19, 825-830.

Manis, M., Houts, P. S. & Blake, J. B. Beliefs about mental illness as a function of psychiatric status and psychiatric hospitalization. *Journal of Abnormal and Social Psychology,* 1963, 67, 227-233.

Maslow, A. H. Cognition of the particular and the generic. *Psychological Review,* 1948, 55, 22-40.

Menninger, K. A. *The vital balance.* New York: Viking Press, 1963.

Metz, J. R. Stimulation level preferences of autistic children. *Journal of Abnormal Psychology,* 1967, 72, 529-535.

NASW opposes delinquency label. *NASW News,* August 1967, 12(4). P. 7.

Novick, J., Rosenfeld, E., Bloch, D. A. & Dawson, D. Ascertaining deviant behavior in children. *Journal of Consulting Psychology,* 1966, 30, 230-238.

Osgood, C. E., Suci, G. J. & Tannenbaum, P. H. *The measurement of meaning.* Urbana: University of Illinois Press, 1957.

Quay, H. The effect of verbal reinforcement on the recall of early memories. *Journal of Abnormal and Social Psychology,* 1959, 59, 254-257.

Rosenthal, R. *Experimenter effects in behavioral research.* New York: Appleton-Century-Crofts, 1966.

Rosenthal, R. & Jacobson, L. *Pygmalion in the classroom: Teacher expectation and pupils' intellectual development.* New York: Holt, Rinehart & Winston, 1968.

Rotter, J. B. Psychotherapy. In P. R. Farnsworth (Ed.), *Annual Review of Psychology,* Vol. 11. Palo Alto, Calif.: Annual Reviews, 1960. Pp. 381-414.

Salzinger, K. Experimental manipulation of verbal behavior: A review. *Journal of General Psychology,* 1959, 61, 65-94.

Sarbin, T. R. On the futility of the proposition that some people be labeled "mentally ill." *Journal of Consulting Psychology,* 1967, 31, 447-453.

Sarbin, T. R. Ontology recapitulates philology: The mystic nature of anxiety. *American Psychologist,* 1968, 23, 411-418.

Sarri, R. C. Organizational patterns and client perspectives in juvenile correctional institutions: A comparative study. Unpublished doctoral dissertation, University of Michigan, 1962.

Schafer, W. E. Deviance in the public school: An interactional view. In E. J. Thomas (Ed.), *Behavioral science for social workers.* New York: Free Press, 1967. Pp. 51-58.

Schafer, W. E. & Polk, K. Delinquency and the schools. In Task Force on Juvenile Delinquency, The President's Commission on Law Enforcement and Administration of Justice, *Task force report: Juvenile delinquency and youth crime.* Washington, D. C.: U.S. Government Printing Office, 1967. Pp. 222-277.

Schwartz, R. D. & Skolnick, J. H. Two studies of legal stigma. *Social Problems,* 1962, 10, 133-142.

Scott, W. A. Research definitions of mental health and illness. In T. R. Sarbin (Ed.), *Studies in behavior pathology.* New York: Holt, Rinehart & Winston, 1961. Pp. 8-22.

Skinner, B. F. What is psychotic behavior? In T. Millon (Ed.), *Theories of psychopathology.* Philadelphia: W. B. Saunders, 1967. Pp. 324-337.

Staats, A. W., Staats, C. K., Heard, W. G & Finley, J. R. Operant conditioning of factor analytic personality traits. *Journal of General Psychology,* 1962, 66, 101-114.

Stuart, R. B. Association between verbal aspects of assessment and successful and unsuccessful casework treatment. Unpublished manuscript, University of Michigan, 1968. (a)

Stuart, R. B. Guide to the planning and evaluation of behavior modification. Unpublished manuscript, University of Michigan, 1968. (b)

Stuart, R. B. Critical reappraisal and reformulation of selected "mental health" programs. Paper presented at First Banff International Conference on Behavior Modification, Banff, Alberta, Canada, April 3-5, 1969.

Szasz, T. S. Criminal responsibility and psychiatry. In H. Toch (Ed.), *Legal and criminal psychology*. New York: Holt, Rinehart & Winston, 1961. Pp. 146-168.

Truax, C. B. Reinforcement and nonreinforcement in Rogerian psychotherapy. *Journal of Abnormal Psychology*, 1966, 71, 1-9.

Verplanck, W. S. The control of the content of conversation: Reinforcement of statements of opinion. *Journal of Abnormal and Social Psychology*, 1955, 51, 668-676.

6

Illustration of Iatrogenic Illness and Its Cure

This chapter will present a very detailed case history, contrasting two completely different approaches to the treatment of a single problem. While it may be hazardous to generalize beyond a single case, it is hoped that the details of the two approaches will illustrate some of the dangers potentially associated with psychotherapy and some of the protections against these dangers inherent in behavior therapy.

Bob was first seen at a special school for emotionally disturbed children at the age of ten. He received treatment oriented to an effort to overcome his "emotional blocks" to eating most foods and to reading. His problems had been present since his early childhood and his unsuccessful treatment at the school extended over an eighteen–month period, five days each week. Because Bob's mother noted no improvement in his problems, she sought behavior therapy for additional assistance. Three behavior therapy sessions were held, and were successful in enabling Bob to show substantial improvement in his two problem areas. This therapy was conducted in a private therapist's office fifty miles from his home. While additional sessions might have been helpful they were not possible because Bob's father, the only driver in the family, was diagnosed as suffering from tuberculosis of the hip several weeks after the third contact.

"Special" Schooling and Its Effects

Before discussing the nature and results of the behavior
therapy offered, the referral materials received from the treatment institution (well after the completion of behavior therapy)
will be discussed in great detail. This detail is included to
illustrate some of the iatrogenic influences which may inter-
fere with psychotherapy premised upon dispositional diagnosis.
At the outset, it should be noted that the treatment institution
is nationally known as one of the finest of its type. The author
of each of these reports is highly respected in his field and in
the professional community in general. The reports reflect a
deep concern with Bob's problems and each therapist's commitment to their amelioration. While it would be incorrect to
generalize from this single instance to the practices of all of
those who seek to modify dispositional features of their patients,
it would not be inaccurate to say that this illustration is typical
of an important segment of such practice.

All of the summaries which were received are reproduced
below. They are presented *exactly as they were received,*
omitting only information that might lead to identification of
the patient, the professionals and the institutions concerned.
The only change made was the addition of numbers in
parentheses in the text of the reports, which correspond to
specific criticisms which will be found in the Critique columns
paralleling the reports.

PSYCHIATRIC REPORT

Text	*Critique*
"We regret that it has taken so long to respond to your [staff of the special school] referral. . . In accordance with your request Bob was scheduled into the	(1) While the presenting problem concerned eating and reading, a medical workup was ordered. It is true that "headaches" were mentioned when Bob was seen by the referral source,

Medical Clinic (1) and was given extensive physical examination and laboratory tests.

"In his physical examination, he looked good to the examining physician, the skull x-ray showed no abnormalities, and his EEG was interpreted as normal (2).

"We saw him in our psychiatric clinic on _____ where he was seen by _____, Child Psychiatrist. We will not review the extensive history which you sent to us, but some of the salient points to make mention were: 1. The significance of the ordinal position of this boy in the family who was born late in this marriage. 2. The caretaking of this boy by a paternal grandmother while the parents both work (3).

"In the interview Bob did not ever look at the examiner directly. His face was always turned away as if he could not expose himself to a direct confrontation with his problems (4). He revealed his interest in aggressive play, particularly hockey, where one would characterize him as a "dirty player" and where he spends a great deal of time in serving penalties (3). His pic-

but these headaches were correlated either with Bob's overeating or being outside in the sun (e.g., fishing) for long periods without a hat.

(2) As indicated in Chapter 5, even implying that a problem does not exist can lead to a negative orientation as though one were "proven guilty by accusation." Having raised the question of physiological problems, the psychiatrist, however obliquely, does suggest medical involvement.

(3) Statements are made, singled out as important, but not elaborated upon. The reader is left with the impression that there are invidious conclusions to be drawn from these items, that they are pathognomonic signs of some grave disorder, but the reader is offered no guidance as to what the conclusions or illness might be. Nor is the relevance of these statements made clear in the light of any systematic diagnostic hypothesis. This might be classed as an illustration of the "incomplete sentence" technique, which is a means of making a statement while metacommunicatively disqualifying the fact that a statement has been made (Watzlawick, 1964).

ture of a person shows a light shaded drawing without hands or feet (3). He describes, and this is supplemented by his mother, some bizarre food habits, which seemed to have been fostered and covertly encouraged by the grandmother (5).

"When [his mother] was seen, she confirmed many of our impressions and observations (3). It was especially significant that Bob had done well with his 3rd grade teacher in spelling and reading and usually does well when she tutors him on Thursday night, but then he fails his test on Friday (3). She also told of his concerns about eating things that had once been 'alive' (3). "In summary, we would describe Bob as a severe characterological problem, with features of anger, passive aggressive qualities (6). We feel that whatever might be the perceptual aspects of his problem (7) are minor as compared with the emotional component (8). Our recommendation would be for Bob to be referred for psychotherapy (9) and with the involvement of the parents as well (9). "Thank you for this interesting referral."

This use of the incomplete syllogism is unfortunately not uncommon in psychiatric and psychological reports.

(4) A metaphorical allusion is made—"as if he could not expose himself to a direct confrontation. . ." Rather than being offered as a clarification of a causal hypothesis, it is offered as a cause. No alternatives are cited. No corroborating evidence is cited. No specific situational referents are included. For example, it would seem important to note that the psychiatric interview occurred at 4 P.M. on a day that included a series of medical examinations which were begun at 8 A.M., and it would also be important to describe the interviewer's behavior in some detail.

(5) An allusion is made to "bizarre" behavior but neither the behavior nor its bizarre characteristics are described. Similarly, pathogenic family influences are mentioned but again not elaborated.

(6) The only direct observational evidence offered is that Bob did not look at the psychiatrist, that he plays what the psychiatrist considers to be a dirty game of knock hockey and he

draws shaded figures with no hands. Nevertheless, Bob has been assigned a far reaching, highly negative dispositional diagnosis. Despite the fact that this is a diagnosis which would be applicable to virtually every segment of Bob's life, there is no reference made to such areas as peer relationships, family relationships, personal hygiene and the very broad range of other activities occurring outside of the examination room.

(7) A problem is introduced in the summary without having been mentioned in the text and one for which no evidence is presented.

(8) Emotional problems have not been described but are definitely defined as severe.

(9) No goals are suggested nor are relevant therapeutic techniques mentioned. It is as though some specific treatment for eating and reading problems would naturally follow from the generalized technology of psychotherapy for characterological problems.

READING EVALUATION

Text

"Bob is a child of average intelligence, who is reading on a second grade level. His comprehension is excellent. His listening comprehension is on a sixth grade level, which is indicative of a child, who, if he could read would be able to work at grade level (1).

"Bob has a poor attitude toward reading (2). His attitude is one of passive resistance (3). However, Bob has difficulty understanding written symbols, with resulting learning problems (4). Bob shows many signs of reversals in his reading. Although Bob knows the sounds of letters in isolation, he is unable (5) to integrate (6) them into his reading. He is unable (5) to use a phonetic approach effectively (4). His spelling is inferior (4). However, with individual help, Bob is able to sound out words (7), but when left on his own he relies completely on visual cues (8).

"As a clinician, I find Bob to have a specific reading disability (8), etiology unknown (9). Is Bob's inability (5) to learn to read caused by a

Critique

(1) This is a useful summary of his successful performance, which might be improved upon only with the addition of more description, supplementing the evaluative and normative conclusions. It would have been helpful, of course, to have also stated his chronological and mental ages, and grade level.

(2) A shift is made from identifying Bob's performance characteristics to stress upon a generalized negative dispositional variable.

(3) Despite further specification of this label, no supporting evidence is supplied. It is implicit that the key to overcoming Bob's reading problem is a solution to his dispositional problem.

(4) A useful performance characteristic is again introduced. It is essential, however, to have an exact description of this deficit, the conditions under which it has been observed, and his response to precisely defined remedial efforts.

(5) The term "unable" is introduced, implying some major obstacle

neurological impairment or neurological maturational lag (10)? There is not much doubt that a primary emotional disturbance can cause a learning block (11), but in Bob's case, I feel that his emotional problems are not the underlying cause (12) but that they only compound the picture."

to acceptable performance. Just as reference to attitudes implies the necessity to overcome dispositional deficits, the reference to abilities implies the need to overcome unspecified structural deficits. It would be far less damaging if the therapist merely referred to what Bob has and has not done, rather than to what he is able or unable to do, as the latter are both void of specific descriptive referents and highly conjectural. Furthermore, to say that he is "unable to read" begs the issue of his therapy, strongly suggesting a negative outcome. According to the logical law of identity, an object cannot be both A and B at the same time (if A is defined as A-not-B). If a child is unable to read, semantically he cannot be expected to be able to read. There is an antitherapeutic finality in this language.

(6) "Integration" is a nonspecific internal process which can be neither observed nor measured. It is inferred from performance and is presumed to change as a function of performance changes. Accordingly, it is superfluous in this context except as a means of continuing an emphasis upon dispositional characteristics. Specification of the performance

would enhance greater clarity.

(7) The exact nature of this help should be detailed as it contains a description of the conditions under which Bob's performance can be improved.

(8) A generalized diagnosis is given which can include a range of problems from illiteracy through a tendency to read semicolons as colons. Furthermore, the data upon which this diagnosis is premised are not cited.

(9) A second obstacle to effective treatment may have been introduced by implication in the notation that the etiology is unknown. There is a common misconception that one must know how an illness developed in order to cure it. This is not necessarily true in medicine and it is totally unsubstantiated in psychology. Indeed, it is doubtful whether most psychological etiological histories are available to a clinician. For example, Quay (1959) has indicated that the recall of early memories may be a function of verbal conditioning, while twin research has shown that the differences in the environmental experiences of twins reared in the same household may be so subtle as to escape notice (Gottesman & Shields, 1966).

(10) A physiological question is raised with no supporting observation. The introduction of this presumptive cause is the third reference to a condition that would materially retard any therapeutic effort. (It is unfortunately not uncommon for etiology to be sought in an arena other than that of a professional who has himself been unsuccessful in treatment.)

(11) This reference to the literature is inaccurate insofar as it presents as uniform an issue about which there is considerable controversy. More importantly, however, it appears to array the forces of science in opposition to Bob's acquisition of higher reading skill. Furthermore, no evidence is offered that might relate this generalization to Bob.

(12) Despite the fact that the etiology is unknown (9), a qualified statement of etiology is made. This unsubstantiated suggestion functions as an additional obstacle to the expectation of improvement.

ARITHMETIC SPECIALIST REPORT

Text

"Bob is working at various levels in arithmetic from third grade to fifth grade (1). There is no evidence of a learning disability in this area (2);—that is, he has no difficulty conceptualizing and understanding number relationships (3). He is working on learning multiplication and division facts now, and the only problem (2) seems to be one of motivation (4) and concentration (3). He dawdles and daydreams (5) and seems to be testing my reactions most of the time (6).

"I have observed that he occasionally reverses numbers. For example, in writing the multiplication table of 8, he wrote 8 x 8 = 46, when he obviously meant 64, all the rest of his work being correct (7). This kind of error is frequently seen, of course, in young children, but in an 11-year-old, it is unusual and may be significant (8)."

Critique

(1) It would be helpful to have description which would supplement this normative evaluation.

(2) The pathology focus of the therapist is revealed in this phrase which also serves to introduce at least mild negative bias in the reader.

(3) Terms such as "conceptualizing" and "understanding" (even though reported as positive) are mental processes which are not observable and therefore are unreliable. They are useless without a description of the data upon which these inferences are based.

(4) Despite the fact that it is the teacher's obligation to "motivate" his students, in this instance low motivation is identified as a deficit of the student. To permit such a shift is to allow the teacher to pass along responsibility for his failure to the student. There is usually little objection to this procedure in settings that stress dispositional diagnoses, as it is typical to ascribe the responsibility of failure to the patient and of success to the therapist.

(5)   While these observations may have relevance for his general classroom demeanor, they hardly shed light upon his arithmetic performance. Their addition to the report, however, offers support for the "second hypothesis"—that is, that Bob is dispositionally defective.

(6)   In addition to the comments in (5), this statement can be questioned because of its peculiarly circular reasoning. While apparently an innocent metaphor—"seems to be testing"—it is in fact a causal statement. It can be outlined as follows:

Premise 1:   Bob dawdles and daydreams.

Premise 2:   (Implied) Dawdling and daydreaming are "testing" maneuvers and teacher is the only person persent to be tested.

Ergo: Bob is testing the teacher.

Proof: Premises 1 and 2.

(7)   This is an excellent observation which is presented in meaningful descriptive detail.

(8) This normative reference is apparently introduced as further evidence of the dispositional deficits of the patient. That it "may be significant" clearly has a negative innuendo. Had it been stated as a problem to be solved, on the other hand, it would have served a very different and useful function.

STAFF CONFERENCE REPORT
(Following four months in the program of the special school)

Text

"Bob is a boy of above average intelligence (1), is 11 years old, white, Lutheran. He is a boy whose social immaturity and unresolved feelings of hostility to adult authority (2) have contributed to an academic disability, particularly reading (3). . . .

"Failure in school has been fairly consistent since the first grade. The lack of remedial reading help and lack of school counseling are crucial factors for consideration (4). Bob shows a negative attitude toward learning and school (2).

Critique

(1) It would be helpful to have great detail in support of this important conclusion.

(2) These are dispositional characteristics for which no evidence is presented.

(3) This is a conclusion which is highly speculative and which is offered as a statement of fact rather than supposition. In addition, it precedes description of academic difficulties and the reader is distracted from concentrating upon a description of the actual problem while attending to the personality problem.

"Physical growth and development have been within the normal range; Bob appears to be in good health. Unusual and bizarre eating patterns exist which are a source of concern and annoyance to the parents, particularly the father (5). Frequent nightmares have occurred in which the mother appears to be in danger in an explosive or bombing kind of situation (6); these have diminished in frequency since Bob has been attending [the school]. There is no known physical cause for the migraine headaches which have been medically diagnosed (7); their presence seems to be indicative of hostility and tension and is a unique disability in children (8). The frequency of these headaches has also diminished (9).

This family is economically stable (1); both parents are regularly employed. The paternal grandmother has been part of the family constellation since before Bob's birth. Three older siblings are married and live elsewhere. The family group is intact with strong familial ties (1). Real love and concern for Bob and his problems have been noted. The parents evidence great anxiety regarding Bob's lack of academic

(4) This is an important observation which includes reference to an essential aspect of the school environment.

(5) "Unusual and bizarre eating patterns" have been mentioned but have not been described. The negative reaction of the parents has been noted but not described. Nor has the school's experience with Bob's eating pattern been described.

(6) The existence of nightmares is cited with some detail, but without an indication of their frequency or the circumstances of their occurrence. It is as though they have pathognomonic significance although we are not told what they signify.

(7) No such headaches are mentioned in the psychiatric report, which apparently summarizes the results of the medical examination.

(8) It is questionable whether either "migraine headaches" or "tension and hostility" are "unique disabilit[ies] in children."

(9) It would be helpful to have some quantifiable data on this subject which would include both the frequency of situations associated with the problem and the frequency of the problem itself.

achievement, his eating habits, the migraine headaches, the manner in which he spends his allowance and his 'careless-ness' (10). The father appears to be quite rigid and holds high and unrealistic expectations for Bob (10); he has projected his own hopes and aspirations onto Bob (11). Father is often impatient and short tempered (10); these attitudes are further complicated by his feeling of being 'too old' and also by a real health problem which may possibly affect his future earning capacities (10). The mother is somewhat overprotective (12). There is a lack of communication between father and son (13), stemming in part from the father's concept of his role as a father (14), his unrealistic expectations and disappointment in Bob (10), and from his low self-esteem (15). All three experience difficulty in handling their anger and frustration (15). Mrs. _____ turns her anger and frustration inward toward herself; Mr. _____ displays hostility to Bob and withdraws himself from situations which do not suit him or which he cannot control and manipulate—he, too, has feelings of hostility toward authority figures (15). Since he has been at [school], Bob has shown aggressive be-

(10) It would be helpful to know not only what behavior prompts the therapist to note that parents evidence anxiety—but also what the parents' specific expectations and reactions to Bob's behavior are.

(11) This is an implied metaphorical statement in which the "as if" has been omitted so that the words appear as a statement of fact. No support is offered for this conclusion, nor are other equally probable alternatives offered.

(12) Because it is so commonplace, this point bears special emphasis. It is said that the mother "*is* overprotective." The word "is" is meant to imply that she acts in an overprotective manner, but as with so many dispositional adjectives, a modifier is transformed into a noun. Furthermore, the word "overprotective" is in no sense unambiguous and requires careful specification.

(13) This statement is contrary to one of the axioms of the interpersonal school: "One cannot NOT communicate [Watzlawick, Beavin & Jackson, 1967, p.2]." (Italics omitted.)

(14) A causal inference is drawn with no evidence indicated,

134

havior and violent loss of self control (5). Bob still finds it difficult to carry through on a task and regresses to an immature pattern of tears or withdrawal when unable to handle peer relationships (15). There is evidence that emotional factors are determing Bob's learning difficulties (15).

"In the brief contacts I have had with the _____ family, certain positive movements forward have been noted (16). The parents have made recognition of the existing problem by the enrollment of Bob at [school] (17); they are amenable to changes in attitude via the casework method, for example Mrs. _____ has changed her method of handling Bob's allowance with a view toward helping him learn through his own experiences and even mistakes; they have seemed to accept the clarification and interpretation of the relationship between anxiety and learning (18) and have eased the pressures at home regarding reading, i.e., Bob is no longer forced to 'read' to his grandmother every night (19). Mrs. _____ has used the casework relationship as an opportunity for the meaningful expression of her feelings and concerns in many personal areas. The opportunity for

other than the introduction of a mentalistic postulate.

(15) A series of dispositional labels is supplied and conclusions are based upon these labels. It is important to note that such conclusions cannot be challenged as they are matters of definition for which no supporting evidence is offered. Each of these statements is in the form of a broad generalization, and no guidance is offered as to the limit of their applicability. Finally, not one of these statements is operationally meaningful; i.e., one would be hard pressed to find a commonly agreed-upon set of referents for such terms, because they cannot be defined in terms setting forth the operations required for their measurement.

(16) It is important to note progress and to keep in mind that events other than psychotherapy may have contributed to such positive changes as have been noted.

(17) Bob was enrolled in the school through his mother's efforts *prior* to the onset of the contacts between the family and the professional staff of the school.

(18) The family would seem to have accepted as clear an issue which the professional community has not fully clarified.

135

ventilation and the psychological support offered seem to be helpful to her, as well as helping her to clarify her own feelings (20). I feel there has been insufficient opportunity to establish a meaningful rapport with Mr. _____ , although I have succeeded in reaching out to him through his wife. Even though Bob verbally expresses negative feelings toward school and learning, it is my impression that he actually desires to learn to read as evidenced by his eagerness for the twice weekly sessions with the reading teacher and his new (21) interest in listening to stories on his appropriate age level (22). Despite a temporary setback, it has been possible to achieve moderately good rapport with Bob—this may be viewed as positive since it is probable that I am somewhat of an authority figure to Bob (23). Bob's low self-esteem seems not to have changed up to this point (5).

"Through casework relationship, efforts should be continued to study Bob in depth (24), to enhance and promote existing ego strengths, and to support the ego weaknesses (25). Peer relationships of a satisfying nature should be encouraged

(19) The parents have apparently been persuaded to forego their efforts to provide Bob with guided practice in the solution to one of his major problems. Such efforts were apparently first negatively labeled as "forced," and pressure may then have been mounted for their discontinuance. Such a decision could conceivably have been warranted on the basis of data, but data were apparently not collected. Indeed it will be shown later that practice of this kind is closely associated with Bob's subsequently improved school performance.

(20) The therapist apparently subscribes to some of the mechanistic metaphors (Adams, 1964) and believes that ventilation which relieves (steam?) pressure is psychologically helpful in some unspecified way. Conversely, however, its iatrogenic effects have also been noted (Schmideberg, 1963).

(21) This statement is very important. Unfortunately, it falls short of precisely identifying the effective reinforcements.

(22) We do not know what type of story he and his grandmother read for the years prior to his

to help strengthen Bob's self-image and feelings of worth in areas other than academic (26). In the academic area, it is felt that achievement should be geared to Bob's abilities and emotional tolerance and readiness (27), with the focus on remedial reading. Care should be exerted to focus here, without over-emphasizing (27) which would cause undue emotional pressures resulting in further feelings of failure (28). The parents may be helped to a fuller understanding of the multiple nature of causality in a learning disability (18); also how the interaction of the family members and the emotional climate in the environment can be factors affecting learning. Mr. _____ appears to be constricted both physically and emotionally (15)—reaching out to involve him in a casework relationship may prove valuable in providing a channel for the ventilation of his feelings (20)—hopefully to improve amenability to some change (29).

starting in the special school. Yet it is implied that this represents a change associated with his treatment.

(23) It would seem improbable that any staff member would not be "somewhat of an authority figure" for a school child. What is its special significance in this context?

(24) Perhaps the last thing which an academically retarded child needs is further study. A boy who is two to three years behind peers in school needs academic help, not diagnosis!

(25) "Ego strengths and weaknesses" have not been identified. Of course, as the *ego* is not observable, it is unrealistic to require empirical evidence to demonstrate its strengths or weaknesses.

(26) There is no information that peer relationships are poor. Furthermore, their relationship to the mentalistic "self-image" might be questioned.

(27) This type of statement usually implies minimal expectations which may, in turn, be associated with a deterioration of performance. Low expectation suggests a willingness to reinforce

minimal performance. When it is suggested that raising expectations could prove harmful, little progress can be anticipated.

(28) A causal statement is made, without qualification, which cannot be proven. At most, a statement of correlation between expectation and performance would be warranted but this, too, would defy quantification and subsequent verification.

(29) A very generalized therapeutic recommendation is made with a comparably vague objective.

FINAL SUMMARY
(Prepared by a Social Worker)

Text		*Critique*
"At the request of Mrs. _____, mother of Bob, we are sending you the following summary of our contacts with Bob.	(1)	This is important information which should be presented in greater detail. There is a faint hint that Bob's mother did not work along with the school but this is not explicit and cannot be refuted.
"Bob attended [school] [for eighteen months] . . . . Contrary to the majority of our students who are referred by a school or an authority in the children's mental health field in the community, Mrs.	(2)	The abilities concept is introduced, implying dispositional obstacles to his development of the necessary skill.

138

_____ sought the enrollment on her own initiative. She was dissatisfied with Bob's progress in the public school and with their attitude toward her and her son (1).

. . . .

"My initial rapport with Bob appeared to be excellent. He came to my office willingly and greeted me warmly when we met in the school (1). He was able to talk about his inability to read (2);—he saw himself as 'dumb' (3). He also discussed his bizarre eating habits, albeit in a flippant manner: 'So what's so terrible about the way I eat?'

"When I asked about the cap he always wore, in and out of the building, he explained that the cap had magical qualities, and he felt it 'prevented bad things from happening to him' (4). He also talked about his dislike of his curly, blond hair. He would prefer to have dark straight hair, and the cap covers his hair (5).

"Since Bob had entered [school] without an evaluation, arrangements were made at [hospital] for a complete physical, neurological and psychological examination (6).

(3) While this is interesting, Bob's descriptions of, rather than his comments upon, his reading problem would be more helpful.

(4) This is a negative observation which has profound pathological overtones. Yet the observation is uncorroborated by others and the psychopathological implications are not made clear.

(5) This concern with cosmetics, while passingly interesting, does not afford useful information. It does, however, subtly suggest another area of pathology without accepting responsibility for so doing.

(6) Neurological and other examinations are ordered apparently before a careful analysis of the presenting problem. Once psychotherapy was recommended, other treatment alternatives were reduced as all therapists were constrained to focus upon psychopathology (Sarbin, 1967).

(7) It is difficult to understand how the term "setting" could provide clarification when the term "hospital" is not understood. This is a good illustration of how professional jargon may be introduced, thereby confusing patients.

"When I discussed the evaluation in advance with Bob, he panicked at the word 'hospital.' I carefully explained that the hospital was merely a setting, like an office (7), where all the testing could be accomplished under one roof, and that he would not be an in-patient. I also told him that one of the major goals of the testing was to help us help him return to the public school as quickly as possible.

"Both Bob and Mrs._____ were distressed by the hospital visits. They both objected to the excessive amount of time they spent waiting for appointments, their dislike of associating with the clinic patients (Negroes and 'poor people'), and the location of the hospital (5).

"When the testing was completed, Bob refused to see me for several weeks. From this reaction, it appeared that as long as I saw Bob on his terms and made no demands on him, he could tolerate me (8). When I made arrangements for the evaluation and insisted that he see them through, he could no longer manipulate me, and I had lost my usefulness to him (8). I became an object which aroused anxiety (9).

(8)   A metaphorical interpretation is made without the expression of an alternative and without supporting evidence. The reasoning here is entirely circular.

(9)   A causal statement is made without qualification on the basis of inferences drawn from a single event. Animistic reasoning is evident in the therapist-to-object transformation.

(10)   Although not contained in Dr. _____'s report, this might have been said, in which case it would have been both quite irrelevant and overly general. Such statements have been shown to have serious iatrogenic effects (Lieberman, 1963).

(11)   One might infer that such a recommendation was made as patients typically do not use this language. If so, it would seem to be totally unsupported, as the psychiatric report made no mention of relevant data. Rather, it has the character of a veiled threat whose implications are onerous for the professions, in that it indicates a tendency of mental health workers to manipulate patients through use of unwarranted conclusions based upon unsupported dispositional diagnoses.

"Mrs._____ was extremely defensive (9) about Dr._____'s meeting with her. She heard him say that Bob was an 'angry young man' (10), and that residental placement may have to be considered (11). She protested that she and Mr._____ had always tried to be good parents and felt they had succeeded in bring up a well behaved young man. I attempted to explain that Bob had never been permitted to be angry externally (12) and that his hostility was forced to become internalized (13). Some of the manifestations of the hostility were the inability to read, the poor eating habits, the migraine headaches and the nightmares (14).

"Although Mrs._____ appeared to understand my interpretation of Dr._____'s findings, she obviously could not accept the treatment plan, intensive psychotherapy, which was recommended (15).

"At this time she appears to be unwilling to return Bob to [school]. She prefers to try the treatment methods proposed by you.

". . .If you have any further questions, please feel free to call upon us at any time."

(12) A statement which has prima facie absurdity (one cannot prevent another from getting "angry externally") and looks like an attempt to justify the veiled threat.

(13) A mechanical metaphor presented as a proven statement.

(14) A causal statement is made declarative despite the fact that it is a virtually untestable supposition.

(15) "Could not accept" is the metaphor for "did not agree with," but cast in dispositional terms it has invidious overtones for the patient. It is another form of professional manipulation of patients through labeling or jargon.

Each of these reports has several features in common with the others. First and most important, the problem was virtually unresolvable from the beginning, owing to the manner in which the diagnosis was phrased. To call Bob a "passive-aggressive character disorder" is to (a) set up grave obstacles to the success of intervention, and (b) disguise rather than elucidate clinical alternatives.

The second common feature of these reports is the general absence of data upon which conclusions are based. Nowhere do the reports contain a statement of the presenting problem, but instead they offer a series of dispositional statements in support of metaphoric conclusions, and use conclusions to support higher order generalizations "as though" the conclusions had in fact been amply verified. This results in a series of spurious conclusions which cannot be refuted, as they are purely definitional in nature.

Third, each of these reports has a strong negative bias, with major emphasis placed upon presumed deficits. Rather than assessing in detail areas of nonproblematic functioning which are construed as building blocks to the achievement of acceptable behavior, these reports concentrate upon identifying obstacles to such programs. Furthermore, many of these obstructions are artifactual insofar as they are entirely presumptive, e.g., neurological, ability and motivational deficits.

Fourth, each of these reports suggests that various observed or inferred behaviors or dispositions are pathognomonic cues of some underlying disturbance, but this disturbance remains unnamed and its other manifestations are unstated.

Fifth, each of these reports either makes sparse mention or entirely omits mention of the conditions under which certain of Bob's behaviors occur or have been noted to change.

Sixth, none of the reports specifies a clear-cut means of overcoming the problem. When therapeutic recommendations are made, they are so general as to be useless. For example, language such as "long-term psychotherapy" not only fails to specify a direction, but it virtually fails to exclude anything, as it might include any technology from total therapeutic noninvolvement to direct physical manipulation of the patient and might include any goal from complete suppression of aggressive behavior to its far-reaching extension.

Finally, despite the vagueness of this treatment plan, *other efforts to overcome Bob's problems were discouraged.* For example, Bob's family was discouraged from working on Bob's reading at home, probably contributing to a deterioration of his performance.

The results of the treatment offered by the school were commensurate with the quality of the summaries upon which it was presumably based. Bob apparently failed to progress in either eating or reading. Eighteen months after the start of treatment, Bob's eating was limited to the same ten foods he ate at the start of treatment. While Bob passed reading at the second-year level when enrolled as a third-grade student in public school, his reading level after completing treatment, as measured by the Wide Range Abilities Test, was 1.6 years. (Unfortunately, no exact data are available for his performance before entering the school.)

There are many speculative explanations for this failure. Based upon the reports that have been furnished, the speculations fall into two major areas. First, it can be assumed that his treatment was not focused upon overcoming his deficit functioning as much as it was focused upon studying his hypothetical characterological problem. Second, it can be assumed that Bob was rewarded for low-level performance and was not strongly encouraged to move to higher levels. Such forward-leading efforts would seem to have been proscribed by the caution that Bob's "emotional tolerance and readiness" not be exceeded. For example, according to his own report, corroborated by his mother, Bob was not required to eat the lunches served by the school but was, instead, permitted to select special foods from among his narrow range of preferences while other children ate the foods on the normal menu.

In addition to failing to progress in areas of great concern, Bob fell further behind the children who should have been his classmates. This, coupled with the fact that he was identified as a student in a school for "disturbed children," contributed a moderate amount of social dislocation.

In summary, then, it can be said that Bob derived little, if any, discernible benefit from attending the special school, as there was no improvement in his eating and reading problems. Furthermore, there is some evidence of his further disengagement from his peers. On the basis of these observations, it can be said that Bob was harmed, on balance, by his contact with the school. Despite the deterioration which should have been evident, it was Bob's mother and not the school that sought alternative solutions to his problem.

Behavior Modification

Presenting problems. The first behavior modification session occurred on April 15 and included Bob, his mother, father, grandmother, and married sister (who did not live in the home but who was obviously quite interested in Bob and was responsible for referring him for behavioral treatment). It was felt important to include all of the relevant family members, as they constitute the salient social environment for Bob and as such provide the resources for changing his behavior. Bob's mother stated two complaints: Bob's failure to eat an acceptable range of food and his failure to read at a grade-appropriate level. She reported that Bob was well-liked by his family and friends and was outwardly very well-adjusted socially. The interaction between all members of the family appeared to bear out the warmth of family ties and Bob's acceptance of and by his family. For example, all four relatives offered highly positive comments about Bob's social behavior and non-academic skills.

Following identification of the presenting problems, it was necessary to gain more specific information. It was established that Bob was permitted to eat only foods of his own choosing both at home and at school. These ten foods were fresh fish, chocolate milk, popcorn, toast, fried potatoes, peanut butter, mushrooms, pizza, steak and pancakes. At home the family capitulated to Bob's breakfast menu choices so as not to delay his leaving for school. Bob arrived home from school at 3 P.M. and his mother regularly left for work at 4 P.M. Because he often ate little at school and because she was concerned that he be certain to eat well, Bob's mother generally prepared foods of his liking for him before she left for work. Bob and his mother typically then ate together, after which Bob enjoyed an evening snack of popcorn and chocolate milk with his father.

To identify his reading deficit, Bob was asked to read aloud. For a sentence printed as follows: "The cat's objective in chasing the dog was merely to tease him," Bob read alone: "This car over in chase this dog was more the to her." Two deficits were obvious. First, the sentence which Bob read aloud made no sense and therefore he obviously did not follow the narrative as he read. Second, he apparently did not visually track the written word; that is, he read the first letter of the word correctly and appeared to either misread or simply make up the word ending. To test the visual tracking problem, it was important to determine whether Bob could correctly identify the words when he knew how they were spelled. Therefore several words were spelled aloud for him. He almost invariably interrupted the word and offered an answer before the word was completed. For example, if the word was "business," the interchange went as follows:

Therapist: B-U-S-I. . . .
Bob: BUS DRIVER!

The spelling test was modified slightly and Bob was told not to answer until told to do so. The second set of interchanges went as follows:

Therapist: B-U-S-I-N-E-S-S (Pause) GO!
Bob: BUSINESS!

Using the modified presentation format, Bob correctly identified more than 25 words of three syllables or more. His correct to error ratio was 1:5 during the first condition but changed to 8:1 during the second condition. The two conclusions which were drawn about his reading deficit were therefore: (1) he was disinterested in the material he read; and (2) he did not visually track the word from beginning to end.

Identification of reinforcers. Having specified the presenting problems, it was next necessary to list reinforcers which could be therapeutically available. In this search, a preference was given for natural versus arbitrary reinforcements (Ferster, 1967; Ferster & Simons, 1966) in the belief that these would (1) have previously demonstrated potency so as to minimize the risk of using a consequence which was not accelerating; (2) be available as they already occur in the environment; and (3) continue to function following therapy, reducing the danger that performance might deteriorate following the fading of arbitrary reinforcement. Specifically, high probability behaviors were sought as prepotent contingencies which could be used to reinforce the lower probability responses of eating a wider range of foods and reading with increased accuracy (Homme, de Baca, Devine, Steinhorst & Rickert, 1963; Premack, 1959, 1965).

The first activity that was described (by Bob's sister) was his interest and proficiency in art work, both in painting and in constructing mosaics. Second, his interest and proficiency in the building of model cars was noted. As a measure of his interest in these crafts, his parents indicated that he spent long hours and worked to perfection on whatever he did (hardly behavior befitting "a severe characterological problem with features of anger, passive aggressive qualities"). Third, his preference for selected late evening (9-10 P.M.) television programs was established, followed by his enjoyment of working with his father at his trade, visiting the family's lake cottage and playing street games with his friends. This list constitutes the resources for change.

A treatment plan for eating changes. As Bob listed his food preferences, it was evident that each food was brown in color, with the exception of pizza which Bob regarded as "brownish" because it tends to darken when cooked and because he ate it with mushrooms. It was suggested, therefore, that Bob begin to introduce some variation in his diet by using a color-coded menu (see Figure 1). He was instructed to choose one new food, at either of the day's home meals, which was not the same as the color of either of the other two main-dish foods served at that meal. For example, if steak and potatoes were on the menu, Bob was required to choose a new food which was neither brown nor white. When he chose a new food, he was to check the box for that particular food on the menu and his mother was then free to serve that food at any subsequent meal. Bob was required to be served initial small (approximately one tablespoon) helpings of all three foods, was allowed to have seconds or thirds, etc., only if he finished the previous helping, and was required to take equal amounts of all three foods.

After eating equal quantities of all foods throughout the day, all agreed that Bob would have sufficient energy to stay up to watch the conclusion (by 10 P.M.) of his 9 P.M. television programs. When he was unsuccessful in eating as prescribed, all agreed that he would lack energy and would therefore be required to be in bed at his normal bedtime, 9:30—midway through his favorite programs.

Color and TV were thus introduced as natural reinforcements, natural insofar as they were drawn from Bob's repertoire and could be logically interrelated with the response to be accelerated. That color was a reinforcer was later supported by his mother's anecdotal observation: As soon as Bob arrived home from the session, he called his friends to ask what color their lunch had been—only he had eaten something purple! For the next several weeks, after-lunch conferences between Bob and his friends began with a review of the color competition among the individual luncheon menus. As a final condition, Bob was required to eat breakfast between 7:30-8 A.M., lunch between 12-1, and dinner between 5:30-6:30.

FIGURE 1

Food Selection Record

COLOR MENU

Instructions: Bob is to choose one food to be added to two to be selected by his mother at each meal. The food chosen by Bob must: (1) be of a different color than either of the foods chosen by his mother; and (2) include at least one *new* food each day.

CHECK IF CHOSEN		CHECK IF CHOSEN		CHECK IF CHOSEN	
	Brown		**White**		**Yellow**
_____	Roast Beef	_____	Bread	_____	Lemons
_____	Veal Roast	_____	Egg Whites	_____	Squash
_____	Pork Roast	_____	Fish	_____	Corn
_____	Lamb Roast	_____	Chicken	_____	Green Grapes
_____	Pork Chops	_____	Potatoes	_____	Onions
_____	Lamb Chops	_____	Shrimp	_____	Bananas
_____	Walnuts	_____	Lobster	_____	Egg Yolk
_____	Pecans	_____	Clams	_____	Cheese
_____	Peanuts	_____	Turkey		
_____	Steak	_____	Oysters		
_____	Chocolate	_____	Cauliflower		**Orange**
_____	Raisins			_____	Oranges
_____	Dates			_____	Acorn Squash
_____	Figs		**Green**	_____	Pumpkin
_____	Mushrooms			_____	Carrots
_____	Peanut Butter	_____	Celery	_____	Peaches
_____	Pancakes	_____	Lettuce		
_____	Pizza	_____	Peas		
_____	Popcorn	_____	Beans		
_____	Hamburger	_____	Spinach		**Purple**
		_____	Broccoli		
		_____	Asparagus	_____	Beets
	Red	_____	Cucumbers	_____	Plums
		_____	Green Peppers	_____	Purple Grapes
_____	Frankfurters	_____	Brussels	_____	Red Cabbage
_____	Tomatoes		Sprouts		
_____	Cherries				
_____	Strawberries				**Blue**
_____	Ham				
_____	Spaghetti			_____	Blue Cheese
_____	Bologna			_____	Blueberries

148

The only other time that food was available was popcorn after dinner, and then only if he had finished all three meals.

Treatment plan for reading changes. The first task was to train Bob in visual tracking. It was decided to use a special apparatus which was to be constructed by Bob and his sister. Bob was instructed to wire a buzzer and a light to one pole of a dry-cell battery and to wire a shielded metal stylus to the other pole. The connecting wires of the light and buzzer were then stapled lengthwise on a large wooden cigar box, exactly one and one-half inches apart. Holes were drilled in one side of the box so that the battery could be placed inside with the lead wires fastened to the signal devices, which were attached to the sides of the box with machine screws. In addition, one toilet paper roller was similarly attached to each end of the box. The wiring was arranged so that when the stylus was placed against the exposed wire on the left side the light would flash, while when the stylus was placed on the wire on the right side the buzzer would sound. (See Figure 2.)

Meanwhile, Bob's sister was asked to type on adding machine tape, triple spaced, all of the words contained in word lists provided as appendices of first through sixth grade readers. A total of 2019 words was listed. The rolls were then fastened to one of the toilet paper rollers with an empty roll fastened to the other roller.

Bob was then instructed to work with one of his parents or his grandmother for 60 minutes per day, divided in a manner convenient to all concerned. He was instructed to touch his stylus to the lead on the left so that the light flashed, then to move his stylus under the word until the buzzer sounded— then he was to pronounce the word aloud. He was to record his own progress with respect to the number of words read correctly after the buzzer sounded, the number of words read correctly before the buzzer, the number of words read incor-

FIGURE 2

Apparatus For Training Visual
Tracking in Reading

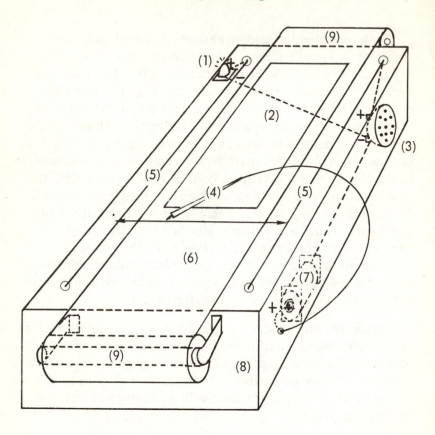

1. SMALL LIGHT
2. CARD covers other words on roll
3. BUZZER
4. STYLUS moves left to right from wire to wire
5. WIRE
6. ADDING MACHINE PAPER ROLL
7. BATTERY
8. CIGAR BOX
9. TOILET PAPER ROLL cut down

rectly after the buzzer, and the number of words read incorrectly before the buzzer. Monetary reinforcement systems were established for two phases of training:

Phase I

Any response made without first flashing the light: no trial
Each word read correctly following sounding of buzzer: 1/10 of 1¢
Each word read incorrectly following sounding of buzzer: no trial
Each word read correctly before sounding of buzzer: 1¢ penalty
Each word read incorrectly before sounding of buzzer: 2¢ penalty

Phase II

Each response made without first flashing the light: no trial
Each word read correctly following sounding of buzzer: 1/10 of 1¢
Each word read incorrectly following sounding of buzzer: 1¢ penalty
Each word read correctly before sounding of buzzer: no trial
Each word read incorrectly before sounding of buzzer: 2¢ penalty

This plan was based upon a seriation of the tasks in training, stressing first visual tracking and then reading accuracy. Visual tracking is not stressed in Phase II as it is implicit in verbal accuracy. An FR 10 schedule (i.e., one point given for each ten correct responses) was adopted for several reasons. First, evidence is available to suggest that such schedules can be used to achieve stable, high rates of responding with developmentally retarded children (Orlando & Bijou, 1960). Furthermore, it was felt that a VR schedule (a point given for a planned but variable number of correct responses), which might have the advantage of maintaining a more stable rate of responding, would be impractical as it would be difficult for Bob's parents to administer. Money was used as reinforcement because Bob purchased his own model cars with money from his allowance, which was previously available on a noncontingent basis. It was felt that model building had demonstrated reinforcing power and could be successfully used in this manner. Finally, the apparatus was used because it was anticipated that a boy with Bob's mechanical interests would find the use of such an apparatus more reinforcing than the use of conventional reading materials.

The decisions with respect to methodology closely parallel the work of others. For example, Wolf and his associates (Wolf, Giles & Hall, 1968) have worked with token reinforcement (redeemable in money) to improve the academic performance of children at the same grade level as Bob. The apparatus employed meets some of the specifications sought by Staats (1968) in similar equipment designed for the study and modification of complex learning in children. This apparatus was simply constructed, easily applied, likely to maintain good experimental behavior over an extended period of time—and its cost was under $4.00.

As a second aspect of his reading program, Bob was required to read aloud to his father or grandmother each evening for 30 minutes before watching television. Time rather than pages read was required because the variety of print size and difficulty would have made standardization of page count arbitrary. The books read were to be of his choosing. His initial selection consisted of books dealing with road racing and auto mechanics.

Results. The changes in Bob's *eating* behavior are recorded in Figure 3. It will be noted that within four weeks the number of foods eaten increased from a baseline of 10 to a total of 35. Three of the new foods he chose during this period (broccoli, asparagus and cauliflower) he subsequently refused to eat. He was therefore denied one evening of late evening television during the first week and two during the fourth week. Reliance upon the color-coded menu was discontinued after the fourth week because it appeared to be superfluous. In an evaluation one year later, it was determined that Bob continued to eat all of the foods cumulatively eaten during the four weeks of observation, in addition to many others. Indeed, he refused to eat only five foods: radishes, broccoli, cauliflower, asparagus, hot cereal of any kind and canned (but not fresh or frozen) vegetables.

There are two measures of *reading* performance which are important here: the accuracy with which Bob read and the relationship between visual tracking and reading. Figure 4 presents the number of words read correctly and incorrectly during the 135 days in which Bob worked with his "reading improvement machine." (Data are presented for every fifth day rather than for an average of five days.) It can be seen that he progressed from a correct/error ratio of 60:44 during the first week to a ratio of 236:4 during the final week. During the first week of the program, Bob expressed great disinterest and hesitancy to work. In a telephone conversation with him, it was established that he was consistently "in the hole" because his errors, while less numerous than his correct responses, were more costly. Therefore he was continuously working to reduce his debt rather than to amass his fortune. Therefore, a new procedure was instituted in which Bob was credited with 25 cents at the start of each session. He was able to credit his winnings and deduct the cost of his errors from this amount. This change was instituted during the fifth session, marked "A" on the graph, and was discontinued at the point marked "B" at session 115.

The only other change in the program occurred at the ninetieth session when Phase II was instituted. While the criterion level for changing from Phase I to II was arbitrarily set at a correct/error ratio of 200:1, Bob appeared to have reached a plateau just below that level and the new program was accordingly instituted. As will be seen from the graph, following 15 sessions of moderately declining performance, his 25-cent "ante" was removed. He then accelerated his performance in order to maintain his accustomed rate of payment. The date for return to school also approached at this time and may have exerted an influence.

It is of interest to evaluate the relationship between visual tracking and the accuracy of Bob's reading. Figure 5 presents a graphic representation of the numbers of correct and incorrect responses associated with complete and incomplete light-read-buzzer cycles. Inspection of the cumulative frequencies

FIGURE 3. Cumulative List of New Foods Bob Selected for Breakfast, Lunch and Dinner Menus

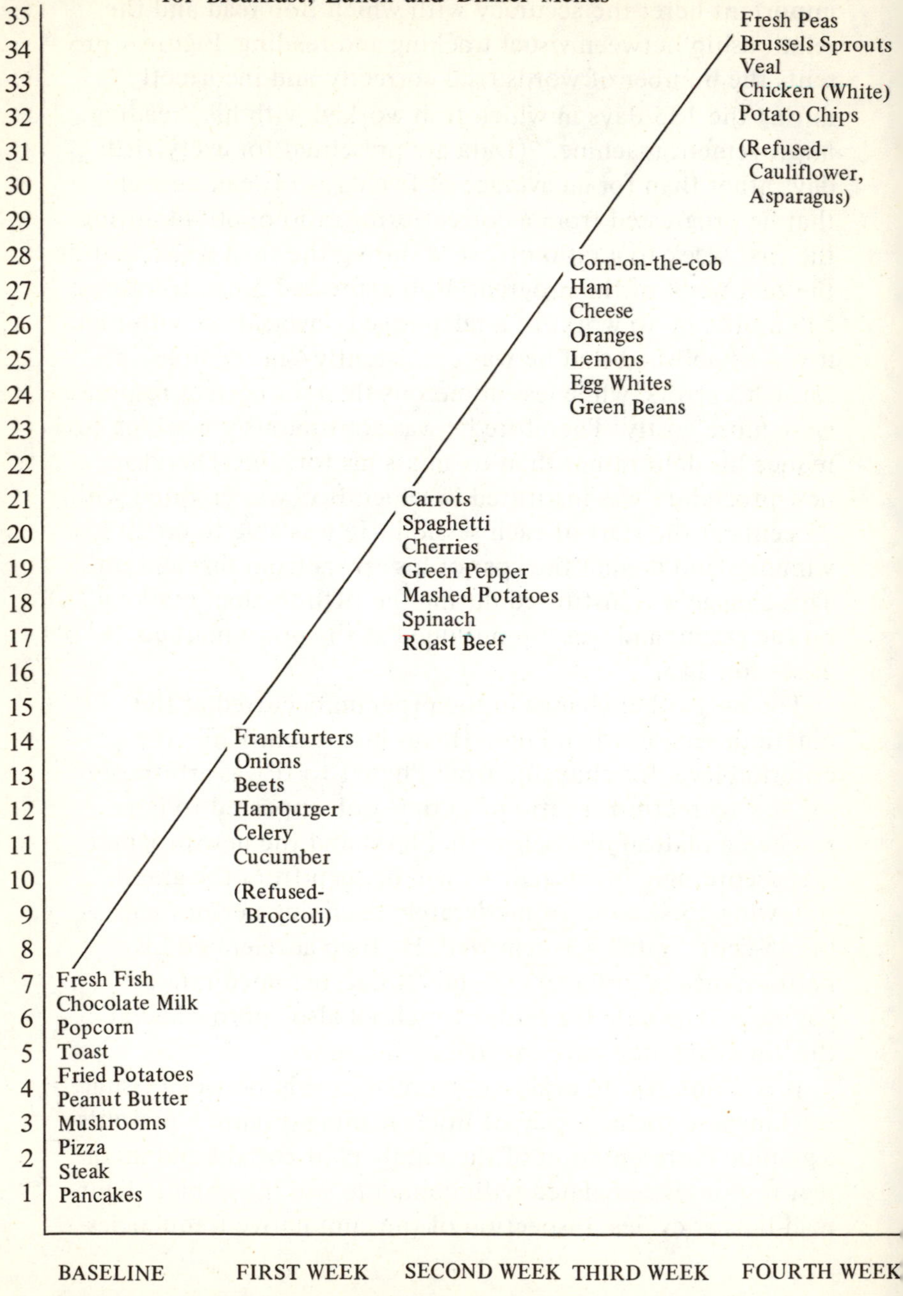

35					Fresh Peas
34					Brussels Sprouts
33					Veal
32					Chicken (White)
31					Potato Chips
30					(Refused- Cauliflower, Asparagus)
29					
28				Corn-on-the-cob	
27				Ham	
26				Cheese	
25				Oranges	
24				Lemons	
23				Egg Whites	
22				Green Beans	
21			Carrots		
20			Spaghetti		
19			Cherries		
18			Green Pepper		
17			Mashed Potatoes		
16			Spinach		
15			Roast Beef		
14		Frankfurters			
13		Onions			
12		Beets			
11		Hamburger			
10		Celery			
9		Cucumber			
8		(Refused- Broccoli)			
7	Fresh Fish				
6	Chocolate Milk				
5	Popcorn				
4	Toast				
3	Fried Potatoes				
2	Peanut Butter				
1	Mushrooms Pizza Steak Pancakes				

BASELINE   FIRST WEEK   SECOND WEEK   THIRD WEEK   FOURTH WEEK

154

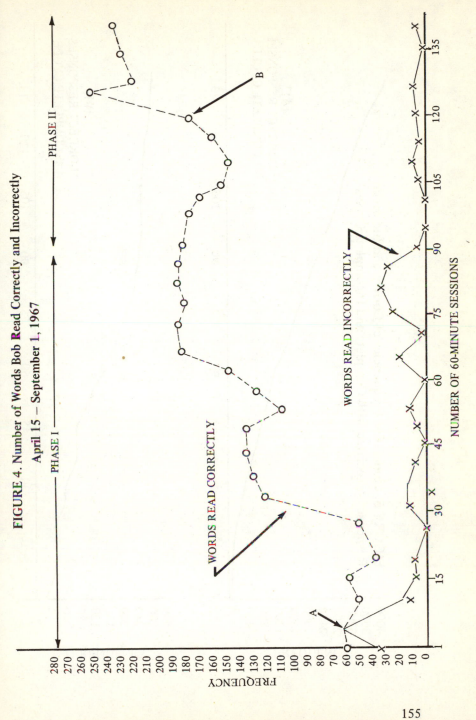

FIGURE 4. Number of Words Bob Read Correctly and Incorrectly
April 15 — September 1, 1967

PHASE I   PHASE II

WORDS READ CORRECTLY

WORDS READ INCORRECTLY

FREQUENCY

NUMBER OF 60-MINUTE SESSIONS

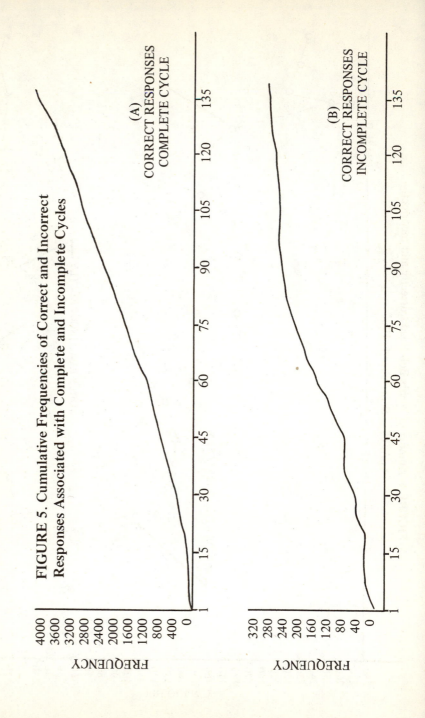

FIGURE 5. Cumulative Frequencies of Correct and Incorrect Responses Associated with Complete and Incomplete Cycles

156

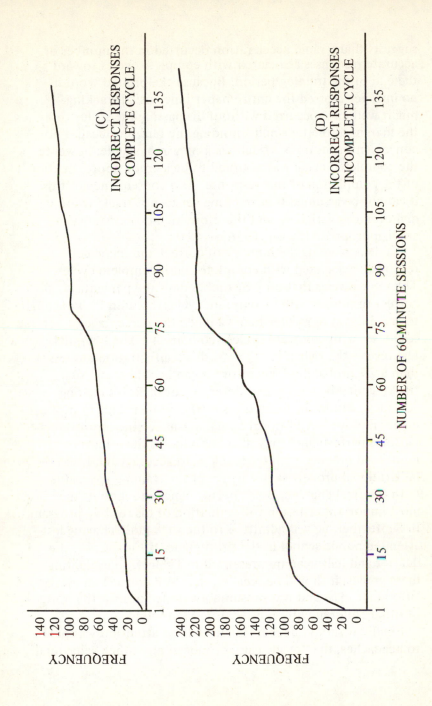

(C)
INCORRECT RESPONSES
COMPLETE CYCLE

(D)
INCORRECT RESPONSES
INCOMPLETE CYCLE

NUMBER OF 60-MINUTE SESSIONS

FREQUENCY

FREQUENCY

suggests that a rapid acceleration occurred in the number of accurate responses associated with complete cycles toward the end of the training period. Because the printed word in no instance crossed the entire paper tape, visual tracking might well have occurred without his passing the stylus to the margin of the tape and sounding the buzzer. Because no convenient measure of visual tracking was available, however, the completed cycle was assumed to be a crude approximation of the completion of this response. As a consequence of this, it cannot be assumed that tracking versus not-tracking are dichotomous variables, and therefore high-power statistics are inappropriate (Siegel, 1956, p. 42).

Table 3 presents the number of correct and incorrect responses associated with complete and incomplete cycles. The table reveals that on 7 of the 28 days the percentage of correct responses with incomplete cycles (column B) was equal to (on 5 days) or greater than (2 days) the percentage of correct responses with complete cycles (column A). The binomial test reveals that when $P = Q = .5$, this configuration has less than a 2% probability. Therefore it can be said that visual tracking may be a necessary determinant of Bob's reading accuracy, within the limitations of the crude means of measurement employed. Additional explanations for the improvement in Bob's performance may also be found in the effects of reinforced practice with feedback as to accuracy, and the motivational properties of the use of the training apparatus.

In the final analysis, Bob's performance in school is the most important criterion for evaluation of his reading program. In September, he was admitted to the fifth grade, having last attended public school in the third grade. His grades for the quarter and half year are presented in Table 4. In evaluating these grades, it should be recalled that Bob entered an average fifth grade class and was presumably graded against the norms of other children with uninterrupted schooling.

Finally it should be mentioned that no attention was paid to headaches, the "magic cap" or indeed any other behavioral problem. One year later, the family continued to regard the treatment as highly successful, although Bob continues to need extra help in academic areas such as spelling.

Discussion. On an interim basis, this case would appear to have been successfully treated through behavior modification therapy. The principal criterion variable will be school performance over time, but at this point Bob has completed one half of a school year and appears to be on an even footing with his classmates.

The total treatment time involved in this case was three sessions, lasting respectively 90 minutes, 60 minutes and 75 minutes. Following the second session, weekly telephone conversations took place until the third session which was scheduled just prior to the opening of public school. At that time, Bob was given a small self-instructional device which would enable him to work through programmed materials. It was hoped that this would aid him in catching up to his classmates' fund of information in subject areas such as social studies, history and science.

Because of the small number of in-person treatment sessions and because the major burden of treatment was carried out in the home, it can be correctly said that the behavior therapist provided guidance to the parents, who conducted the actual treatment. Similar procedures have been followed in work with a wide range of behavioral disturbances in children (Harris, Wolf & Baer, 1964; O'Leary, O'Leary & Becker, 1967; Patterson, 1967; Risley & Wolf, 1967; Thomas, Becker & Armstrong, 1968; Wahler, Winkel, Peterson & Morrison, 1965). Such treatment can be broadly classified as "intervention therapy" in the terms used by Kanfer and Phillips (1966). The treatment occurred in the natural environment, where unskilled persons were trained in operant conditioning in order to use a broad spectrum of essentially natural reinforcers to increase the frequency of certain classes of objectively defined responses.

It is unfortunate that this treatment was not conducted under the rigorous conditions necessary for the investigation

TABLE 3

Number and Percent of Correct and Incorrect Responses with Complete and Incomplete Cycles

Day		Cycle Complete		Cycle Incomplete	
		Correct Response (A)	Incorrect Response (C)	Correct Response (B)	Incorrect Response (D)
1	N	39	10	21	30
	%	80	20	41	59
5	N	48	19	16	45
	%	72	28	26	74
10	N	45	3	7	18
	%	94	6	28	62
15	N	36	4	0	4
	%	90	10	0	100
20	N	51	0	0	0
	%	100	0	0	0
25	N	97	8	27	10
	%	92	8	73	27
30	N	130	9	5	9
	%	94	6	36	64
35	N	118	6	20	1
	%	95	5	95	5
40	N	131	0	9	0
	%	100	0	100	0
45	N	110	2	0	5
	%	98	2	0	100
50	N	108	3	20	10
	%	97	3	66	33
55	N	129	0	19	5
	%	100	0	79	21
60	N	160	8	28	18

	%	100	0	100	0
70	N	171	4	18	19
	%	98	2	49	51
75	N	174	10	17	23
	%	95	5	43	57
80	N	179	16	14	12
	%	92	8	54	46
85	N	179	1	13	0
	%	99	1	100	0
90	N	180	0	9	0
	%	100	0	100	0
95	N	180	0	6	0
	%	100	0	100	0
100	N	180	3	4	2
	%	98	2	66	33
105	N	164	7	0	1
	%	96	4	0	100
110	N	154	4	1	1
	%	97	3	50	50
115	N	161	0	5	3
	%	100	0	63	37
120	N	179	0	2	4
	%	100	0	33	66
125	N	244	3	10	1
	%	99	1	91	9
130	N	225	3	0	3
	%	99	1	0	100
135	N	233	1	2	0
	%	99.5	.5	100	0

TABLE 4
Bob's First- And Second-Quarter Grades
Fifth Year Public School

Subject	Grades			
	First Quarter		Second Quarter	
	Grade	Effort	Grade	Effort
English	B	B	C	A
Handwriting	D	B	D	A
Literature	C	B	C	A
Reading	C	B	C	A
Spelling	C	B	C	A
Arithmetic	C	D	C	C
Science	B	B	B	A
Social Studies	B	B	B	B
Art	A			A
Physical Education	A			A
Library	C			C
Music: General	B			B
Auditorium	C			C

of causal relationships. While the major dependent variables
(eating, reading accuracy, and school performance) are simply
stated and objectively measurable (Terrell, 1958), the independent variables (the operant techniques and school training) are
both complicated by the uncontrolled aspects of social interaction. For example, Rosenthal and Jacobson (1966) have
demonstrated that teacher expectation can have a profound
impact upon student performance. (Indeed, this difference
alone might be sufficient to explain Bob's radical improvement in school.) Furthermore, while own-control or A-B-A
designs are available for research on a single subject (Browning,
1967; Paul, 1967), these designs were unfortunately not
purposefully employed. Therefore the conclusions drawn
from this treatment must be qualified as tentative statements
of association.

Finally, it may be instructive to explain how 18 months
of treatment by a number of professionals could have resulted
in deterioration while three sessions of behavioral therapy
could have been followed by substantial improvement. It can

be postulated that three factors interrelated to promote Bob's deterioration while at the school: (1) he was misdiagnosed; (2) based upon the erroneous diagnosis, improper treatment was prescribed; and (3) as a corollary to improper treatment, other adaptive efforts were discouraged. At the risk of repetition, each of these points will be discussed in greater detail.

Bob was diagnosed by the staff of the school as suffering from a characterological problem based upon a small sample of his behavior and apparently without any attempt to identify the situational concomitants of his problematic responses. A common consequence of removing a problem from the context of its occurrence is a tendency to replace parsimony with complex and often irrelevant theorizing.

A very vivid demonstration of this error and its effect has been provided by Ayllon and his associates (Ayllon, Haughton & Hughes, 1965). Using cigarettes as a reinforcer, they conditioned a schizophrenic inpatient to pace up and down the day room while holding a broom. Two psychiatrists were then invited to observe this patient's behavior and comment upon their observations. Their comments were couched in metaphors of symbolism and their analysis stressed a schizoid disturbance. If her behavior were deemed harmful and if they sought to overcome her pacing-with-a-broom behavior through curing her schizoid personality, their treatment would have been at least long-term and at worst totally unsuccessful at no cost to themselves and at a high cost to the patient. If instead they sought to overcome it by removing the reinforcement, they might have expected rather dramatic and immediate results. The authors offer the following conclusion:

> The etiology of many so-called psychotic symptoms exhibited by hospitalized patients or those in need of hospitalization does not have to be sought in the obscure dynamics of a psychiatric disturbance. Symptoms may be the result of an accidental pairing of the peculiar behaviour with some form of reinforcement meted out by the unsuspecting environment [Ayllon, Haughton & Hughes, 1965, pp. 5-6].

The elaborate explanations of the school staff therefore overlooked one of the most elemental and ubiquitous principles of human behavior: that responses will be influenced by their consequences (Skinner, 1938). By extension of this principle, it can be assumed that even unwanted responses are maintained by their consequences (Skinner, 1948), and that their control must be sought through the manipulation of external events.

The second source of deterioration is the probability that the form of treatment resulting from the dispositional diagnosis was harmful in its effect. This analysis of the treatment must unfortunately be overly general as the original treatment recommendations were essentially void of detail. Each of the recommendations, however, can be said to have reduced the chances that the disorder could be successfully treated by attributing its etiology and manifestations to areas beyond the control of Bob or others in his immediate environment. This had the effect of shifting the focus of attention from that which is directly manipulatable (the environment) to that which is neither directly manipulatable nor well understood (Bob's presumed dynamics). Once the disorder was reified and efforts expended to resolve the "underlying disturbance," deterioration was a likely outcome. This was necessitated by the fact that the very treatment techniques introduced to overcome the dispositional problem worked to exacerbate the behavioral problems. Unfortunately, one cannot "feed an unready ego" and deprive a food manipulator at the same time. As long as the former course was pursued, the behavioral problems could be expected to worsen.

If the treatment recommendations had stressed a change in the salient problem-maintaining features of the environment, they would have been specific and it would have been possible to train salient members of the environment to work to Bob's advantage. Because the locus of the problem was removed from the social environment and placed in the inner reaches of Bob's character, sources of extratherapeutic help were discouraged.

Unfortunately for Bob, this shift in the conception of his problem also removed it from the realm of treatability by the professionals involved at that time. This is a consequence of the fact that there is no empirically validated means of modifying inner dispositions, while the technology for the change of behavior is freely available (Homme, 1967).

Summary

A case has been presented to demonstrate failure and deterioration associated with psychotherapy, followed by rapid progress associated with behavior therapy. The failure is seen in the fact that the patient made no change in his eating behavior. The deterioration in reading was not well-established because of the unavailability of standardized measurement of the patient's reading skill at the start of psychotherapy. The deterioration of the patient's social position with respect to his peers is clearly demonstrated as he was further behind the scholastic level of his age mates following psychotherapy than he was at its beginning. Furthermore, judging from their decision to withdraw Bob from treatment, it is apparent that Bob's parents also perceived psychotherapy as ineffective.

The unfortunate results of psychotherapy can be attributed to the failure of the psychotherapists to identify the exact nature of Bob's problems and then to formulate a plan appropriate to their removal. The patient was diagnosed as suffering from "characterological" problems rather than as suffering from "eating" and "reading" difficulties. As Sarbin (1967) has indicated:

> The sentence, 'a child. . .is known to have tendencies toward severe (mental) illness. . .' contains implications different from 'a child has tendencies to hit other children' [p. 447].

The psychotherapists posed for themselves the task of overcoming a personality defect as a means of achieving a behavior-change end. Because no technology is apparently available for changing personalities, their effort was unsuccessful.

In contrast, the behavior therapist posed for himself the task of overcoming two behavioral problems which were related to environmental events, through a process of behavioral assessment. Once the relevant aspects of the situation were established, it was possible to modify these and thereby to change conditions under which Bob responded. From a change in these conditions, behavior change followed naturally.

Apart from comparing the results of the two approaches, several other comparisons are instructive. First, while psychotherapy was ineffective after eighteen months, behavior therapy was effective in three sessions. It would obviously be imprudent to expect long-term psychotherapy to consistently fail, just as it would be imprudent to expect behavior therapy of such short duration always to be effective. Yet it should be obvious from the models upon which the two approaches are premised that these outcomes can often be predicted with relative safety. Second, it should be clear that the two approaches differ markedly in their reliance upon objective data as a basis for both planning and evaluating treatment. The close monitoring of change inherent in behavior modification treatment should afford a major protection for patients against the dangers of erroneous therapeutic maneuvers.

Finally, the two approaches can be differentiated on the basis of the logic used by each. The terms of psychotherapy make frequent reference to psychic structures (e.g., "character" or "ego"). While these terms are better used as "process variables" (i.e., as states rather than as structures), their use in even this capacity is contingent upon verification of many assumptions which are still unscientific in character. In contrast, the logic of the behavior modification approach is quite explicit and each step in its chain of reasoning is verifiable through making selected changes and evaluating their effectiveness. Furthermore, because of the non-assumptive character of the approach, its essential elements can be taught to patients, who are then in a position to assist therapists in promoting desired changes.

References

Adams, H. "Mental illness" or interpersonal behavior? *American Psychologist,* 1964, 19, 191-197.

Ayllon, T., Haughton, E. & Hughes, H. B. Interpretation of symptoms: Fact or fiction? *Behaviour Research and Therapy,* 1965, 3, 1-7.

Browning, R. M. A same-subject design for simultaneous comparison of three reinforcement contingencies. *Behaviour Research and Therapy,* 1967, 5, 237-243.

Ferster, C. B. Arbitrary and natural reinforcement. *Psychological Record,* 1967, 17, 341-347.

Ferster, C. B. & Simons, J. Behavior therapy with children. *Psychological Record,* 1966, 16, 65-71.

Gottesman, I. I. & Shields, J. Contributions of twin studies to perspectives on schizophrenia. In B. A. Maher (Ed.), *Progress in experimental personality research,* Vol. 3. New York: Academic Press, 1966. Pp. 1-84.

Harris, F. R., Wolf, M. M. & Baer, D. M. Effects of adult social reinforcement on child behavior. *Young Children,* 1964, 20, 8-17.

Homme, L. E. A behavior technology exists—here and now. Paper presented at the meeting of the Aerospace Education Foundation, Washington, D.C., September 1967.

Homme, L. E., de Baca, P. C., Devine, J. V., Steinhorst, R. & Rickert, E. J. Use of the Premack principle in controlling the behavior of nursery school children. *Journal of the Experimental Analysis of Behavior,* 1963, 6, 544.

Kanfer, F. H. & Phillips, J. S. Behavior therapy: A panacea for all ills or a passing fancy? *Archives of General Psychiatry,* 1966, 15, 114-128.

Lieberman, A. The case of the meek matriarch. *Journal of the Indiana State Medical Association,* 1963, 56, 315-321.

O'Leary, K. D., O'Leary, S. & Becker, W. C. Modification of a deviant sibling interaction in the home. *Behaviour Research and Therapy,* 1967, 5, 113-120.

Orlando, R. & Bijou, S. W. Single and multiple schedules of reinforcement in developmentally retarded children. *Journal of the Experimental Analysis of Behavior,* 1960, 3, 339-348.

Patterson, G. R. Reprogramming the social environment. *Journal of Child Psychology and Psychiatry,* 1967, 8, 181-195.

Paul, G. L. Strategy of outcome research in psychotherapy. *Journal of Consulting Psychology,* 1967, 31, 109-118.

Premack, D. Toward empirical behavior laws: 1. Positive reinforcement. *Psychological Review,* 1959, 66, 219-233.

Premack, D. Reinforcement theory. In D. Levine (Ed.), *Nebraska symposium on motivation.* Lincoln: University of Nebraska Press, 1965. Pp. 123-188.

Quay, H. The effect of verbal reinforcement on the recall of early memories. *Journal of Abnormal and Social Psychology,* 1959, 59, 254-257.

Risley, T. R. & Wolf, M. M. Experimental manipulation of autistic behaviors and generalization into the home. In S. W. Bijou & D. M. Baer (Eds.), *Child development: Readings in experimental analysis.* New York: Appleton-Century-Crofts, 1967. Pp. 184-194.

Rosenthal, R. & Jacobson, L. Teachers' expectancies: Determinants of pupils' IQ gains. *Psychological Reports,* 1966, 19, 115-118.

Sarbin, T. R. On the futility of the proposition that some people be labeled "mentally ill." *Journal of Consulting Psychology,* 1967, 31, 447-453.

Schmideberg, M. Iatrogenic disturbance. *American Journal of Psychiatry,* 1963, 119, 899.

Siegel, S. *Nonparametric statistics for the behavioral sciences.* New York: McGraw-Hill, 1956.

Skinner, B. F. *The behavior of organisms.* New York: Appleton-Century-Crofts, 1938.

Skinner, B. F. "Superstition" in the pigeon. *Journal of Experimental Psychology,* 1948, 38, 168-172.

Staats, A. W. A general apparatus for the investigation of complex learning in children. *Behaviour Research and Therapy,* 1968, 6, 45-50.

Terrell, G. The need for simplicity in research in child psychology. *Child Development,* 1958, 29, 303-310.

Thomas, D. R., Becker, W. C. & Armstrong, M. Production and elimination of disruptive classroom behavior by systematically varying teacher's behavior. *Journal of Applied Behavior Analysis,* 1968, 1, 35-45.

Wahler, R. G., Winkel, G. H., Peterson, R. F. & Morrison, D. C. Mothers as behavior therapists for their own children. *Behaviour Research and Therapy,* 1965, 3, 113-134.

Watzlawick, P. *An anthology of human communication.* Palo Alto, Calif.: Science and Behavior Books, 1964.

Watzlawick, P., Beavin, J. H. & Jackson, D. D. *Pragmatics of human communication.* New York: Norton, 1967.

Wolf, M. M., Giles, D. K. & Hall, R. V. Experiments with token reinforcement in a remedial classroom. *Behaviour Research and Therapy,* 1968, 6, 51-64.

7
Rx for Change: Behavior Assessment

Of the many different approaches to diagnosis and treatment of "mental illness," the techniques of behavior assessment and modification are the ones most likely to be successful. To understand why, it is necessary to first examine the alternative diagnostic approaches and note their distinguishing features. After discussing the implications of various types of diagnosis and assessment, the techniques of behavior assessment will be discussed in greater detail.

Models of Diagnosis and Assessment

In large measure, the character of any diagnostic approach is determined by the nature of the situations in which it is to be applied. Diagnostic approaches may differ in their basic theoretical assumptions, their taxonomic structure, the scope and source of their data, and the nature of the inferences and predictions which are yielded by their categories.

At one end of the spectrum are the sociologically oriented approaches. These taxonomies are intended to serve as means of classifying broad sectors of the population in order to determine which social services are needed. These taxonomies must assume that behavior, whether acceptable or unacceptable, is fundamentally under social control; they must be concerned with molar units of behavior; they must typically depend upon demographic or self-report data; and their categories must be used to make predictions of group versus individual behavior.

At the other extreme are taxonomies which are intended to serve as a basis for individual treatment planning. These approaches assume individual or social controls of behavior, may depend upon observational or self-report data, and must yield individual versus group predictions. Because the requisites of these two taxonomic systems are at variance, their applications must be differentiated.

The general clinical taxonomic system of the American Psychiatric Association apparently ignores this distinction and must be viewed as an effort to achieve the objectives of both approaches in a single instrument. For example, a man may be classified as a "schizophrenic." This would place him in a category of persons believed to be in need of extensive treatment. It would not, however, indicate whether he will cut off his ear and yet paint modern French masterpieces, suffer from fits of overwhelming depression and yet write great Russian novels, or engage in uncontrolled paroxysms of motor and vocal activity and vegetate in the back ward of an American mental institution. In short, assignment of an individual to a clinical diagnostic category indicates (at least in principle) that he shares certain behaviors with other individuals so diagnosed, but it does not shed light upon other socially productive aspects of his behavior, the etiology of his problems or potential strategies for the solution of his problems. Therefore clinical diagnosis serves neither of its masters well.

Beyond clinical diagnosis, there are several additional approaches to the description of human distress, each drawing upon a somewhat different theoretical orientation. For example, different systems might emphasize one or more of the elements represented in Figure 6 as major sources of observed behavior. It might be assumed that body chemistry is fundamentally responsible for mood state, which determines social experience. On the other hand, exactly the opposite set of relationships might be hypothecated, and it might be assumed that social experience is the major etiolog-

**FIGURE 6. Relationship Between Overt Behavior
and Individual and Social Forces**

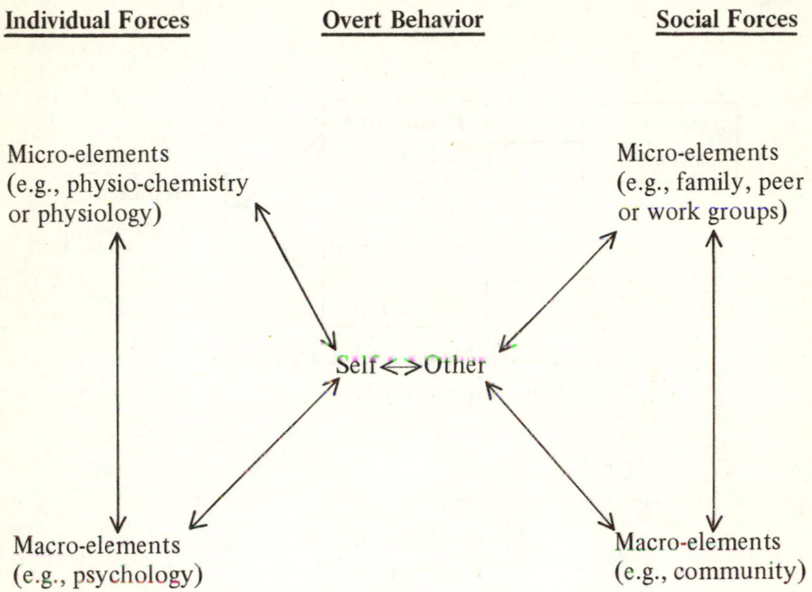

Individual Forces   Overt Behavior   Social Forces

Micro-elements
(e.g., physio-chemistry
or physiology)

Micro-elements
(e.g., family, peer
or work groups)

Self <-> Other

Macro-elements
(e.g., psychology)

Macro-elements
(e.g., community)

ical factor in physiological disturbances. If it is assumed that
the relationship among these variables must proceed in only
one direction (e.g., if it is assumed that physiological
processes determine social behavior while social experiences
have virtually no effect upon physiology), then adherents of
the first approach would be bound to seek psychophysiolog-
ical sources of behavior control, while adherents of the latter
approach would be bound to seek socio-environmental
sources of behavior control. It is of great importance to
determine exactly which set of relationships is expected to
prevail and to generate intervention strategies accordingly, if
behavior change efforts are to have cogency and consistency.

Once this decision is made, the clinician is required to
select from among the varied models which are represented
in Figure 7. Three of these models have been developed by

FIGURE 7. Four Models of Scientific Psychology

(A)

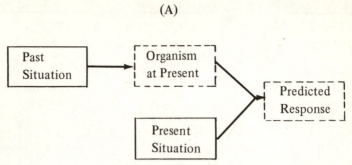

Cronbach's model for prediction
from historical data

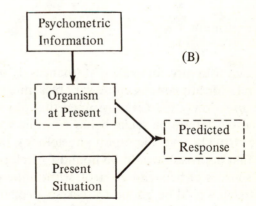

(B)

Cronbach's model for prediction
from ahistorical data

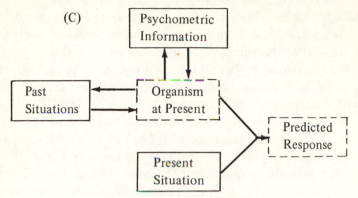

(C)

Cronbach's united model for
prediction from historical
and ahistorical data

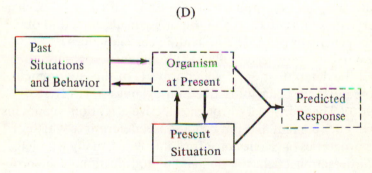

(D)

A model for behavioral prediction

Cronbach (1957) and contrast the role of historical (A and C) and ahistorical (B) data in approaches which do (B and C) and do not (A) include psychometric data. In each of Cronbach's models, however, the present situation is recognized as a force upon the predicted behavior which is essentially parallel to the force exerted by the individual.

In the behavioral model (D), the individual is recognized as exerting an important influence upon both his past and present situations rather than being the passive recipient of these situations. This distinction is necessitated by three factors. First, operant behavior is defined as a set of responses to or operations upon the environment in order to bring about some change in the environment (Skinner, 1938). The change which is produced may be only a momentary redistribution of reinforcement or it may be an endurable change in the manner in which reinforcements are apportioned. If response classes are understood primarily in terms of their effect upon the environment, then it is clearly essential to formalize in theory the practical reciprocity between the behavior of an individual and his environment. Second, the behavioral model must deny an isomorphism between the actual physical characteristics of a situation and the individual's detection of these characteristics. The individual certainly does not respond to every aspect of an environmental configuration, and the determination of which aspects of the environment do control his behavior is an empirical question (Terrace, 1966). The individual, through selective attention, shapes his own environment and thus, in a sense, determines which of its properties have relevance for him. Third, many problems of interactional behavior demand a modification in the problematic behavior of the individual in advance of and as a necessary condition for changes in the behavior of others.

For example, Stuart (1969a, 1969b) has pointed out that when one party to a dysfunctional marriage seeks relief from marital conflict, he must secure the desired changes by first modifying his own behavior. This implies that he is at least partially responsible for the conflict situation as it exists rather than being the passive victim of its demands. Therefore his relationship with his immediate situation must be understood to be reciprocal. If this were not the case, the spouse who sought treatment would have a virtually hopeless plight as the relief of his discomfort would depend upon changes in the behavior of his spouse and this would be, *ipso facto,* clearly beyond his control.

In addition to postulating that the individual and his environment are reciprocally related, the behavioral model presented here does not include psychometric data. The individual is identified in coarse terms such as name, age and objectifiable achievement, but his covert response tendencies are not described. This stress upon observable behavior and exclusion of inferences concerning inner state has been termed "nonsense" by Bakan (1968), who argues that "except in a limited number of latter-day, die-hard hyper-disciplined studies, most investigators regard the observations of their studies only as a basis for inference about other things [p. 85]." Apart from being pejorative, this statement intimates that it is implicit in most descriptive studies that predictions of certain classes of observable future events may be based upon reliable descriptive data. Thus, testable inferences are made from observable events to future observable events. In no sense, however, is it essential that inferences be drawn to inner states, and as the data in Chapter 4 have indicated, chaotic conditions result when this is done.

Behavior Assessment Scales

Numerous systems of behavioral ratings have been developed for use by clinicians (Lyerly & Abbott, 1965), including such commonly used systems as those developed by Phillips and Rabinovitch (1958), Zigler and Phillips (1960), Wittenborn (1955), and Piercy and Overall (1968). Each of these systems stresses the observation of behavior by several clinicians, the factor analysis of these observations and the identification of second or higher order groupings of these observations. As an example, Piercy and Overall (1968) factor-analyzed clinician ratings based upon the Brief Psychiatric Rating Scale (Overall & Gorham, 1962) and found four major functional systems of behavior: thinking disturbance, which includes disorganization, unusual thought content, hallucinations and disorientation; psychomotor activation, which includes agitation-excitement and withdrawal-retardation; direction of agression, which includes extrapunitiveness and intropunitiveness; and mood, which includes depression and elation. This approach, along with the system developed by Phillips, Broverman and Zigler (1966), is closely analogous to the types of judgments which are commonly rendered in clinical diagnoses. The limitation in all of these approaches is their stress upon pathological functioning and neglect of acceptable behavior. This approach is likely to yield a harmfully biased description of the patient.

In contrast to these pathology-oriented systems, Patterson (in press) has developed a means of assessment in which specific classes of children's behavior are observed in a neutral orientation, with ratings of health and pathology following a second-order analysis of the observations. This approach has considerable merit, owing to the range of observations upon which it draws and to its independence of potentially problematic labeling effects.

Bechtel and Patterson (1968) have developed this notion further. They assert that one can postulate the existence of "states" or "class[es] of observable responses with emission rates which covary over situations within a single person [p. 5]." Thus the initial behavioral observations can be used to support a second order judgment concerning the state of the individual or the probability that he will act similarly in varying situations. These state assumptions, in turn, may be used to infer "traits" which refer to "a set of state values observed over several situations [p. 5]." Thus, observable behaviors can serve as the data for probabilistic inferences which are testable bases for predictions of the behavior of a particular individual in several different situations.

Unlike the studies of dispositional diagnostic procedures which were reviewed in Chapter 4, ratings of behavioral assessment tend to enjoy very high interjudge reliability (Wright, 1960). For example, Ulmer and Lieberman (1967) developed a Children's Minimal Social Behavior Scale which consists of 31 items in the form of: "E. sits and says, 'How are you?' Score + any discriminable response to this question _____. Score + if response is verbal and appropriate _____ [p. 10]." The authors report that correlation coefficients for pairs of observers ranged from .97 to .99, which implies near identical ratings by observer pairs. Therefore it can be concluded that there is considerable potential safety in the use of these systems, from the standpoint of reliability.

Validity, it will be recalled, is concerned with the question of whether the instrument measures what it is intended to measure. Each of the behavioral rating scales tends to show a positive correlation. For example, the Wittenborn (1955) scales have been shown to correlate with psychiatric diagnosis and with the outcomes of varied radical treatments offered to psychotic patients, while the Brief Psychiatric Rating Scale (Overall & Gorham, 1962) was shown to correlate with psychiatric diagnosis and the outcome of drug treatments. A more important measure of the comparative validity of psychiatric diagnosis and behavioral ratings was provided by the Brink, Oetting and Cole study (1967), in which it was shown that while psychiatric diagnosis did not serve to provide accurate predictions of the outcome of work placement programs, at least one-half of all of the behavioral rating items did serve as a basis for accurate prediction.

In view of these findings, it can be concluded that behavior assessment scales are at least as useful as, and may yield considerable advantages above, diagnostic approaches that depend upon inferred dispositional states. The behavioral ratings may have greater reliability and validity and in addition can be made more value free and may be more readily taught to observers who do not have professional training. This is a particular advantage to clinical programs administered in institutional settings in which nonprofessionals outnumber professionals by a considerable margin.

Situational Factors as Internal Elements in Behavior Assessment

There are at least two main reasons for the need to include a description of situational factors in behavior assessment, one deriving from the nature of measurement and the other from the clinical uses to which the assessments are put. On the measurement side, it is clear that if the response being rated is objective and measurable—e.g., a man running—multiple observers are likely to reliably agree about what is taking place. But if the validity of the judgments is also to be assessed, it is of vast importance to identify the conditions that control his behavior. For example, Ferster (1965) has suggested:

> A complete moving picture record of a 'man running down a corridor' provides enough data for only a minimal classification of the behavior. The man could be running because someone is chasing him. The man could be running because the train will leave in ten minutes from a distant station. The man could be running because he has just won a sweepstake prize. All these behaviors are closely similar to each other topographically, yet they are examples of extremely diverse kinds of behavioral control [pp. 9-10].

If one wished to modify the man's running behavior, it would be essential to manipulate the controlling conditions. The strategies which would be used to do this would be very different if he were running from a pursuer or toward a train. In addition, predictions of future running behavior would be accurate only to the extent that they also made reference to the controlling conditions.

The clinical ramifications of the failure to indicate controlling conditions have been pointed out in a paper by Ayllon,

Haughton and Hughes (1965) which was cited in Chapter 6. The authors worked with a 54-year-old female mental patient who was given cigarettes for pacing the floor while holding a broom. Two psychiatrists were asked to view her behavior through a one-way-vision mirror. The authors report:

Dr. X described the patient as follows:

'The broom represents to this patient some essential perceptual element in her field of consciousness. . .it is certainly a stereotyped form of behaviour such as is commonly seen in rather regressed schizophrenics and is rather analogous to the way small children or infants refuse to be parted from some favourite toy, piece of rag, etc.'

Dr. Y made these comments about the same patient:

'Her constant and compulsive pacing, holding a broom in the manner she does, could be seen as a ritualistic procedure, a magical action. . . .Her broom would be then: (1) a child that gives her love and she gives him in return her devotion, (2) a phallic symbol, (3) the sceptre of an omnipotent queen. . . . this is a magical procedure in which the patient carries out her wishes, expressed in a way that is far beyond our solid, rational and conventional way of thinking and acting [p. 3].'

At the simplest level, if one wished to predict whether she would continue carrying the broom, one need only assess the probability of her continuing to receive cigarettes. This would require assessment of the nurses and attendants who distributed cigarettes to her. At a more complex level, it would be necessary to speculate about the nature of an unobservable and untestable "psychotic process." If one wished to undertake treatment, a knowledge of only the inferences contained in the psychiatric report would suggest the need for arduous and ineffective psychotherapy, while a knowledge of the controlling conditions would suggest a rather elementary behavior modification strategy.

Forces in the environment in which behavior occurs function both as conditions which control that behavior and as factors which contribute to the process whereby actions are evaluated as acceptable or unacceptable. This is implicit in the assessment process insofar as this process is oriented to making decisions concerning the disposition of the patient. For example, Erikson (1964) has argued that "deviance can be defined as conduct which is generally thought to require the attention of social control agencies [p.11]," and Goshen (1962) indicates that the outcome of the deviance definition process is the simple determination of whether or not the deviant will be included or excluded from the general community. Goshen suggests that the range of situations about which deviance decisions are made is broad, including, at one extreme, whether or not a deviant should be institutionalized, through whether he should be given or allowed to retain employment, to whether he should be granted a pension or a deferment from military service, at the other extreme.

It is important to note that the offense of the deviant does not necessarily involve injury to the larger community (Erikson, 1964). For example, an individual's hallucinations may have absolutely no bearing upon the well-being of the group. At times the hallucinatory individual may be heralded as a religious leader or artist of distinction while at other times he might be accorded the ignominy of mental patient status (Hoffer, 1960; Medlicott, 1958). Whether he is visited with riches or ruin as a consequence of his behavior will in large measure be dependent upon the prevailing values of his community rather than its wish for protection from an intrinsically pernicious influence.

In evaluating patient behavior, it is essential to specify both the controlling conditions and the criteria that have been applied in evaluating it as deviant. The values of the larger society are unclear and inconsistent in many areas and the degree of predictability quickly vanishes as the number of social subgroups proliferates. Therefore, in viewing a child who walks only on the heels of his feet, it is essential to know: how he has been rewarded for this behavior, and whether he has been encouraged to walk on his heels to preserve his shoes or to strengthen his leg muscles, rather than to stave off the advances of the devil. It is very easy and yet perilous to lose sight of both of these factors when confronted with unusual patterns of behavior. Judgments about mental health problems are relativistic judgments, which therefore must include clear specification of the situational determinants of behavior if sophistry is to be avoided.

A Framework for Behavior Assessment

Above and beyond the requirement that the system must demonstrate reliability and validity, a clinically useful framework for assessment must possess four other features. First it must conclude with statements that are patient-specific. Merely labeling a patient in accordance with a taxonomic system does not describe the unique characteristics of his assets and liabilities. Merely identifying features of the patient's behavior does not reveal the unique conditions that control his behavior. Therefore clinical assessment must be ideographic rather than nomothetic; that is, it must describe the unique features of his behavior rather than merely indicate which actions he has in common with others in a similar grouping (contrary views are expressed by Patterson, 1965, and Wilson, 1963).

In addition to stressing observations of the unique features of the patient's behavior and the contexts in which it is likely to occur, the framework must also rely upon descriptive language with a low level of abstraction. Colby (1967) regarded the psychiatric classification system as "a majestic absurdity [p. 1]" because of its chaotic language. He therefore adopted this view and premised his system upon "everyday descriptive definitions [p. 2]."

Language should serve as an aid to the cogency of the clinician's thinking rather than as an obstacle. Terms such as "counter-cathexis," "libidinal vicissitude," or "ego" are based upon extended chains of untested and untestable inferences. This results in confusion of processes with states and structures. These terms are removed from rather than keyed directly into intervention procedures and therefore they get in the way of clinical assessment. In their place, simple phenomenological descriptions would be far more useful.

A third requirement for frameworks of assessment is that they should describe acceptable behaviors as fully as they describe unacceptable behaviors. Constructive behaviors are likely to be more numerous and more socially important than unacceptable behaviors. In addition, a far greater array of more powerful techniques is available for the acceleration of desired behaviors than is available for the deceleration of undesired behaviors. Isaacs, Thomas and Goldiamond (1961) have said:

> Experimental laboratory work indicates that it is often extremely difficult to eliminate behavior; extinction is extremely difficult where. . . .reinforcement has been irregular, as it is in most of our behaviors. . . Experimental laboratory work has provided us quite readily with procedures to increase responses [p. 91].

Since the range of techniques which can be used to build upon acceptable behaviors is greater than the range available for eliminating unacceptable responses, it is of great importance to include mention of positive response repertoires in behavior assessment.

A final requirement of clinically useful frameworks is that they must be parsimonious. They must include only such information as is necessary for effective decision-making. In a great many instances it is possible to successfully treat patients for problems whose etiologies are unknown. For example, identification of the precise learning history that might be held accountable for Bob's (Chapter 6) failure to use visual tracking in reading was not an essential prerequisite of effective treatment. Time spent in collecting such a history would have been unproductive for several reasons.

First, Freud himself (1946, pp.60-61) came regretfully to the conclusion that patients' accounts of past events tended to be based more upon fantasy than upon fact. It is therefore doubtful that one can ascertain the veracity of many possibly relevant historical events. Second, those events which are accurately recalled may in fact be irrelevant to the presenting complaint. For example, many mothers who seek treatment for their children at child guidance clinics attribute to "harsh words from a second grade teacher" problems that may have been elicited and maintained by parental responses at home. Unfortunately, there is no way of testing the relevance of any such history. Finally, a knowledge of history may be irrelevant precisely because history is not reversible. If in fact behavior problems were elicited by a teacher's harsh words, nothing can be done to alter this fact. Furthermore, the knowledge of an adverse history may itself create a negative bias in the clinician (as mentioned in Chapter 5) which may foreclose valid therapeutic opportunities to the patient.

In addition to limiting the amount of etiological material, parsimony would also impose curbs upon the scope of cross-sectional descriptive detail. Kanfer and Saslow (1965, in press) have suggested two frameworks which are very broad in scope. Each of the schemes calls for information in seven categories:

1. Initial analysis of the problem situation
2. Clarification of the problem situation
3. Motivational analysis
4. Developmental analysis
5. Analysis of self-control
6. Analysis of social relationships
7. Analysis of social-cultural-physical environments

The major advantage of these systems is their comprehensive stress upon the situational events associated with the occurrence of carefully defined problematic responses. The major limitation of the systems is their broad informational requirement. It is unlikely that clinicians would have access to or much use for details in such a broad spectrum.

An alternative system. For illustrative purposes, a framework for assessing voluntary (operant) behavior will be discussed, a system adapted from a more complete outline of behavior assessment which is available elsewhere (Stuart, 1968). This system begins with a precise specification of problematic behaviors. First, the units of behavior must be identified in operationally meaningful, observable terms.

Phrases such as "impulsive," "immature" and "passive" must not be used, for they are not words which communicate descriptions of the problematic behaviors—they simply contain information about how an observer evaluates the actions. For example, one observer might term an adolescent's approach to a strange girl at a bus stop as "impulsive" while another might give it a much more positive label such as "assertive." While there is danger of absurd reductionism in response to the demand for behavioral specificity, it seems to be essential to stress the use of language that has objectifiable meaning.

The reason for beginning assessment with problematic responses is that this approach offers some guidelines as to how an assessment approach can be focused and narrowed. Without a problem description as a point of departure, the clinician would be faced with the imponderable task of sampling all classes of an individual's behavior. With a focal problematic response, the inquiry can be restricted to the affected and immediately relevant areas. For example, Bob's (Chapter 6) habits of self-care and personal hygiene were not relevant to his eating and reading difficulties and data was not collected in these areas.

In describing problematic behavior it is essential to identify the nature of the environment in which it occurs, including the events that are antecedent and consequent to the problematic behavior. In this manner, data is collected to fill in the detail germane to the following paradigm:

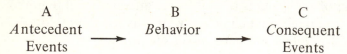

A	B	C
Antecedent Events	Behavior	Consequent Events

The environment must not be regarded as a static phenomenon. Ferster (1965) has described the environment as "a set of those practices that are contingencies applied to particular forms of behavior [p. 11]." Some of the environmental stimulation precedes or is antecedent to responding while other stimuli follow or are the consequences of responding. There are at least four classes of antecedent stimuli, or stimuli which set the occasion for responding. The first class of stimuli has been termed *"instructional"* by Goldiamond (1968, p. 27), and these refer to the rules or set of the subject as directed by the behavior modifier. For example, Bob was instructed to attend to the light and sound cues from his reading device. The second class of stimuli provide the subject with information concerning the probability with which he can expect to be reinforced for emitting a response. Some events are termed *"discriminative stimuli"* and indicate that reinforcement is likely to follow a particular response. Other events, termed *"stimuli delta,"* indicate that reinforcement will not follow as a consequence of responding. Both sets of stimuli gain their behavior-controlling properties through the subject's prior experience of responding in their presence. Bob, for example, was trained to expect reinforcement following his reading a correct word after the appearance of the light, and he was trained not to expect reinforcement for correct responses which were not preceded by the light.

A third class of antecedent events has been termed *"potentiating variables"* by Goldiamond (1968, p. 27). These variables are procedures which are undertaken in order to assure the effectiveness of a reinforcement. For example, depriving Bob of his allowance increased the importance of the money he could earn through correct reading responses which were rewarded. Finally, a fourth class of antecedent events may be termed *"facilitating stimuli."* These are the tools which are essential prerequisites for the occurrence of the response. For example, Bob could not be expected to read words that were not made available to him nor to respond to visual and auditory cues that were not provided.

Just as there are four classes of antecedent events, four classes of consequent events can be identified. The term "consequent events" is reserved for those events produced by the response. When Bob read words correctly under the appropriate stimulus conditions, he received credit for a fraction of a cent. He did not produce the money by reading but he did bring the money under his own control. After he read a word correctly, his watch also may have sounded a click. His reading did not produce the click and therefore the sound is *not* regarded as a consequence of his reading—reading and clicking were merely a pair of coincidental events.

The first class of consequent events is *positive reinforcement.* A positive reinforcer is an event that leads to an increase in the rate of responding when it is contingent upon (produced by) a particular response. It has been called "reward," but this term should be used cautiously to avoid the implication of a subjective state of pleasure, which is not necessarily associated with positive reinforcement. Many events function as positive reinforcers for an individual, and a complete catalogue is impossible because events gain and lose control rapidly. For example, apple pie might be a positive reinforcer for a hungry man but might be a very aversive stimulus for the man who has just risen from a banquet table. Because this is true, there are virtually no reinforcers that can be categorized as universal positive reinforcers which have potency at all times. Therefore, when functionally analyzing the behavior of an individual according to the A-B-C paradigm, it is essential to closely observe not only the consequent event but also its effect upon the patient's rate of responding.

If the patient's response rate rises or is maintained following the presentation of a consequence, the event is clearly a positive reinforcer. If the individual's behavior decreases following the presentation of a class of consequences, these stimuli must be regarded as *aversive events.* These are events that function to depress response rates. They are sometimes called "punishment," but in using this term one must be careful to avoid the subjectivism implied in the "pain" which is presumed to result from punishment, for not all aversive stimuli are painful. Like positive reinforcers, aversive events are highly variable from person to person and for the same person at different times. For example, a severe lashing with a heavy belt may appear to be a clearly aversive event. However, it can only be defined as aversive after its functional properties have been studied and the following question has been answered:

Does the behavior which results in this consequence decrease following the consequence? If the beating is associated with the only parental attention a neglected child receives, it may come to serve as a positive rather than aversive consequence.

A second type of consequence which leads to a decrease in the rate of responding is termed an *"extinguishing event."* These events are totally neutral with respect to a behavior which was previously maintained by positive reinforcement. It is their neutral character which accounts for the decreased rate of response. For example, if Bob's parents simply stopped giving him money for reading at the early stage of his self-treatment and began ignoring his responses when he was asked to read word lists that were devoid of narrative, it is quite likely that he would have stopped reading them.

The fourth class of consequent events has been termed *"negative reinforcement."* When negative reinforcement occurs, an aversive event is withdrawn following the emission of a desired behavior. For example, Bob's mother might have nagged him constantly to read, stopping only when he began to work. Nagging would be an aversive event which was terminated or withdrawn when the desired response occurred and therefore "negative" can be contrasted with "positive" reinforcement in which an event is presented following a response.

The varied types of antecedent and consequent events and their effects are summarized in Table 5. This table does not exhaust the possibilities for consequences because rather complex paradigms are possible. All of these more complex paradigms, however, depend upon one or more of the elements mentioned. In selecting consequences to manipulate, several important considerations must be borne in mind. Positive reinforcement involves the provision of a stimulus which, by definition, is attractive to the patient. As a result of being associated with positively reinforcing events, the therapist may himself become more positive for the patient, who may then be inclined to follow his directives more closely (Goldstein, Heller & Sechrest, 1966, pp. 73-211). In addition, the therapist has precise control over the emergent response because he can narrowly specify the range of responses for which positive reinforcement is given. In contrast, while the therapist still has control over the emergent response, negative reinforcement has the disadvantage of associating the therapist with negative events. This may decrease his control over the patient, who may even avoid therapeutic encounters entirely because of the therapist's aversiveness.

The manipulation of aversive events has proven to be a highly effective procedure for use in laboratory settings (Azrin & Holz, 1966), but it is subject to many disadvantages in natural living situations. First, the punisher like the dispenser of negative reinforcement is likely to be avoided by his subject, reducing his effective behavior control. Second, in stressing the reduction of problematic responses, the behavior modifier loses control of the response that occurs in its place. For example, if a father stressed stopping his son from throwing his ball against a wall for excitement, he might run the risk of seeing his son throw his baby brother downstairs for similar excitement. Third, many conditions must be met in the effective use of punishment (Azrin & Holz, 1966). For example, every time the problematic response occurs it must be punished. If some responses are not punished but are instead allowed to meet with positive reinforcement, they will be far more difficult to eliminate. In addition, punishment must be delivered with relative immediacy and severity, requirements which impose practical and ethical limitations. Furthermore, punishment must be delivered independently of any positive reinforcement. As the delivery of punishment is commonly associated with intense attention and emotion, there are certain social reinforcements for the patient inherent in the punishing situation. Finally, punishment commonly interrupts any learning situation significantly. For example, while a child cries loudly after being scolded for spilling his orange juice, he is unlikely to be willing to obediently pick up his spoon and eat like a "big boy."

The use of extinction to reduce problematic responses is

also subject to more problems in natural settings than are encountered in laboratory contexts. Like punishment, extinction does not provide the behavior modifier with close control over the response that he intends to replace the response that has been eliminated. In addition, it is frequently difficult or impossible to apply extinction to socially disruptive or self-injurious behaviors. For example,

TABLE 5

Functional Properties of Antecedent and Consequent Events

I.   To accelerate or increase the rate of behavior

    A. Present or modify the following antecedent events:

       1. Instructional stimuli (or rules)
       2. Discriminative stimuli (or indication that positive reinforcement will be offered)
       3. Potentiating variables (or variables which ensure that reinforcers will be positive)
       4. Faciliating stimuli (or tools)

    B. Present or intensify the following consequent events:

       1. Positive reinforcement
       2. Negative reinforcement

II. To decelerate or decrease the rate of behavior

    A. Present or modify the following antecedent events:

       1. Instructional stimuli
       2. Stimuli delta (or indications that positive reinforcement will not be offered)

    B. Remove or modify the following antecedent events:

       1. Potentiating variables
       2. Facilitating stimuli

    C. Present or intensify the following consequent events:

       1. Extinguishing (or neutral) events
       2. Aversive (or punishing) events

a boy who speaks out in class is likely to be positively reinforced by peers while his teacher vainly seeks to extinguish his behavior, and a mother can hardly ignore her child's running headlong into busy streets. Finally, extinction is often problematic because following the withdrawal of a positive reinforcer, the patient is likely to temporarily increase the rate of his problematic behavior in an apparent effort to regain the lost positive reinforcement. This temporary acceleration of negative responding is likely to be hazardous.

In conclusion, it can be said that the use of positive reinforcement has considerable advantage over the use of negative reinforcement, punishment or extinction. This suggests that a central treatment strategy in a large number of instances must be the acceleration of acceptable responses which will take the place of (or provide an alternative means of achieving the positive reinforcement which presently results from) unacceptable behaviors. Once the desired behavior is accelerated, decelerating strategies may be useful in eliminating the problematic responses.

These considerations lead to the major paradigm of assessment. It calls for identification of the antecedent and consequent events for both acceptable and unacceptable behavior, as summarized in Table 6.

From this analysis of the controlling conditions of both sets of responses, it is possible to identify which antecedents and consequences of acceptable behavior must be applied and which antecedents and consequences of unacceptable behavior must be eliminated. Ideally it should be possible to make the consequences of existing problematic behaviors the consequences of the desired acceptable behaviors. For example, an adolescent who earns money from the sale of stolen hubcaps might be given an opportunity to earn the same amount of money through acceptable employment. Whether or not this is possible, treatment will be successful only if the balance between positive and aversive consequences is more favorable following acceptable responses than it is following problematic responses.

TABLE 6

Paradigm for Behavior Assessment and Case Planning

Environmental Stimuli (including the behavior of others)	Patient Behavior	
	Desired Response Specify _____	**Problematic Response** Specify _____
Antecedent Events — Missing Stimulation	Instructional _____ Discriminative _____ Potentiating _____ Facilitating _____	Instructional _____ Stimulus Delta _____
Antecedent Events — Present Stimulation	Instructional _____ Discriminative _____ Potentiating _____ Facilitating _____	Instructional _____ Discriminative _____ Potentiating _____ Facilitating _____
Consequent Events — Missing Reinforcement	Positive _____ Negative _____	Extinguishing _____ Aversive _____
Consequent Events — Present Reinforcement	Extinguishing _____ Aversive _____	Positive _____ Negative _____

Two implications of this approach should be made explicit. First, the existence of problematic responses is explained in terms of the reinforcement that follows these responses. By the same token, the failure of acceptable behaviors to appear is explained in terms of the insufficiency of the events that would have stimulated them and/or the reinforcements that they produce. In this sense, neither the occurrence of problematic responses nor the nonoccurrence of acceptable responses is considered to be coincidental or a function of the individual's "inner state." By excluding accidents, problems can be considered in a rational manner; by excluding inner states, therapist subjectivism is held to a minimum while emphasis is placed upon that which can be accomplished. These consideratons lead to the second implication of the approach, which is that the environment and not the individual is basically in control of the individual's behavior. If the individual is to change, someone in the environment must instruct, signal and facilitate the change while modifying the potentiated consequences of behavior. It is hardly possible for the individual to change himself. This suggests that intervention procedures which are oriented to changing the individual alone, rather than to changing the environment and the individual combined, have a limited chance of success.

Following from the fact that manipulation of the environment is an essential prerequisite to behavior change, it is essential to gain control of the immediately relevant aspects of the environment. In working with Bob, for example, it was first necessary to gain his parents' cooperation, for they, and not the therapist, were responsible for stimulating and reinforcing his eating and reading behaviors. Similarly, a counselor cannot modify the classroom behavior of a student but must work with the teacher to promote desired changes.

When the patient is an adult, he may be the primary source of information pertaining to the occurrence and change of problematic behaviors. When the patient is a child, others in the environment must often provide this information. The most basic data concern the rate at which behaviors occur, because all behavior modification undertakings are concerned with changing the rate of responses (i.e., increasing the rate of acceptable behaviors while decreasing the rate of problematic behaviors). Other data pertain to the manner and contexts in which the response takes place. Without this information, the therapist would be denied measures of the initial magnitude of the problem or of the effect of his efforts. The most suitable format for keeping this record is graphing, which affords immediate visual feedback about the effectiveness of an intervention technique. Samples of useful graphs can be found in Chapter 6 (Figures 4 and 5).

Behavioral specificity and graphing of behavior change are vital elements in the process of self-correction which characterizes the behavior modification approach. When intervention is planned, behavior change hypotheses are constructed. The hypotheses take the form of: "If Bob is permitted to watch television between 9:30 and 10:00 P.M. following his eating three full meals, then he will extend the range of foods which he eats." This hypothesis is testable by comparing the rate of his eating before intervention with the rate of his eating after the contingency has been applied. Information derived from this assessment practice can be used to justify continuation, modification or termination of a treatment technique. As the data are recorded on a daily basis, it is possible to make immediate adjustments in the techniques used. These adjustments might call for the intensification, reduction or total replacement of specific procedures, and the effects of these changes are subjected to a repetition of the same close scrutiny.

When this close attention is paid to patient behavior, both therapist and patient are afforded a large measure of protection against iatrogenic illness. When monitoring is not possible, as with dispositional diagnoses which stress unobservable inner states and lack refutable hypotheses, both the therapist and the patient face the risk of iatrogenic illness. As has been indicated throughout this book, these harmful effects of treatment may not be ascribed to willful malice but, rather, they are the probable consequences of efforts to undertake behavior change without sufficient data about the nature of the presenting problem or the ongoing effects of treatment.

Summary

Behavior assessment has been shown to be a highly reliable and valid assessment procedure. Its advantages over dispositional diagnosis are its immediate relevance to a particular patient, its objectivity, its stress upon acceptable as well as problematic behaviors, and its parsimony. Because it does not draw heavily upon past history or nonobservable personality traits, it is relatively free from sources of error which are associated with extended chains of inference. Above all, behavior assessment is a highly practical undertaking because completion of its Antecedent-Behavior-Consequence paradigm provides information which is immediately relevant to treatment. Finally, it makes available objective data at the start of and throughout the treatment process, and these data serve as a major means of evaluating the effectiveness of treatment and safeguarding the patient from any potential iatrogenic effects.

References

Ayllon, T., Haughton, E. & Hughes, H. B. Interpretation of symptoms: Facts or fiction. *Behaviour Research and Therapy,* 1965, 3, 1-7.

Azrin, N. & Holz, N. C. Punishment. In W. K. Honig (Ed.), *Operant behavior: Areas of research and application.* New York: Appleton-Century-Crofts, 1966. Pp. 380-447.

Bakan, D. *On method.* San Francisco: Jossey-Bass, 1968.

Bechtel, G. G. & Patterson, G. R. States, traits and situations. Mimeo, Oregon Research Institute, Eugene, Oregon, 1968.

Brink, R. W., Oetting, E. R. & Cole, C. W. Technical research report number X: Predicting post-hospital outcome of psychiatric patients. Unpublished manuscript, Mental Health and Manpower Project, Colorado State University, 1967.

Colby, K. M. Computer-aided language development in nonspeaking mentally retarded children. Technical Report CS 85, 1967, Stanford University Computer Science Department, School of Humanities and Sciences.

Cronbach, L. J. The two disciplines of scientific psychology. *American Psychologist,* 1957, 12, 671-684.

Erikson, K. T. Notes on the sociology of deviance. In H. S. Becker (Ed.), *The other side: Perspectives on deviance.* Glencoe, Ill.: Free Press, 1964. Pp. 9-23.

Ferster, C. B. Classification of behavioral pathology. In L. Krasner & L. P. Ullmann (Eds.), *Research in behavior modification.* New York: Holt, Rinehart & Winston, 1965. Pp. 6-26.

Freud, S. *An autobiographical study.* London: Hogarth Press and Institute of Psychoanalysis, 1946.

Goldiamond, I. Programs, paradigms, and procedures. In H. L. Cohen, I. Goldiamond, J. Filipczak & R. Pooley, *Training professionals in procedures for the establishment of educational environments: A report on the CASE Training Institue (CTI).* Silver Spring, Md.: Educational Facility Press–IBR (Institute for Behavioral Research), 1968. Pp. 27-28.

Goldstein, A. P., Heller, K. & Sechrest, L. B. *Psychotherapy and the psychology of behavior change.* New York: Wiley, 1966.

Goshen, C. E. Therapeutic implications of diagnosis. In J. H. Masserman (Ed.), *Current psychiatric therapies,* Vol. 2. New York: Grune & Stratton, 1962. Pp. 8-18.

Hoffer, A. Abnormalities of behavior. In P. R. Farnsworth & Q. McNemar (Eds.), *Annual review of psychology,* Vol. 11. Palo Alto, Calif.: Annual Reviews, 1960. Pp. 351-380.

Isaacs, W., Thomas, J. & Goldiamond, I. Application of operant conditioning to reinstate verbal behavior in psychotics. In T. R. Sarbin (Ed.), *Studies in behavior pathology.* New York: Holt, Rinehart & Winston, 1961. Pp. 88-92.

Kanfer, F. H. & Saslow, G. Behavioral analysis: An alternative to diagnostic classification. *Archives of General Psychiatry,* 1965, 12, 529-538.

Kanfer, F. H. & Saslow, G. Behavioral diagnosis. In C. Franks (Ed.), *Assessment and status of the behavior therapies and associated developments.* New York: McGraw-Hill, in press.

Lyerly, S. B. & Abbott, P. S. *Handbook of psychiatric rating scales.* Washington, D.C.: Public Health Service Publication 1495, 1965.

Medlicott, R. An inquiry into the significance of hallucinations with special reference to their occurrence in the sane. *International Record of Medicine,* 1958, 71, 664-677.

Overall, J. E. & Gorham, D. R. The Brief Psychiatric Rating Scale. *Psychological Reports,* 1962, 10, 799-812.

Patterson, G. R. Some problems involved in the classification of deviant children. Paper presented at the Peabody Symposium on Classification, Nashville, 1965.

Patterson, G. R. An empirical approach to the classification of disturbed children. *Journal of Clinical Psychology,* in press.

Phillips, L., Broverman, I. K. & Zigler, E. Social competence and psychiatric diagnosis. *Journal of Abnormal Psychology,* 1966, 71, 209-214.

Phillips, L. & Rabinovitch, M. Social role and patterns of symptomatic behaviors. *Journal of Abnormal and Social Psychology,* 1958, 57, 181-186.

Piercy, D. C. & Overall, J. E. Minimum adequate description of psychiatric disorder. In American Psychological Assoication, *Proceedings of the 76th Annual Conference of the APA.* Washington, D.C.: American Psychological Association, 1968. Pp. 475-476.

Skinner, B. F. *The behavior of organisms.* New York: Appleton-Century-Crofts, 1938.

Stuart, R. B. Outline for behavioral analysis and case planning. Unpublished manuscript, University of Michigan, 1968.

Stuart, R. B. Operant-interpersonal treatment for marital discord. *Journal of Consulting Psychology,* 1969, in press. (a)

Stuart, R. B. Token reinforcement in marital treatment. In R. Rubin (Ed.), *Proceedings of the second annual meeting, Association for Advancement of the Behavioral Therapies.* New York: Academic Press, 1969, in press. (b)

Terrace, H. S. Stimulus control. In W. K. Honig (Ed.), *Operant behavior: Areas of research and application.* New York: Appleton-Century-Crofts, 1966. Pp. 271-344.

Ulmer, R. A. & Lieberman, M. The Children's Minimal Social Behavior Scale (CMSBS): A short objective measure of personality functioning (10 yr. level). Paper presented at the meeting of the California State Psychological Association, San Diego, 1967.

Wilson, R. S. On behavior pathology. *Psychological Bulletin,* 1963, 60, 130-146.

Wittenborn, J. R. *Manual: Wittenborn Psychiatric Rating Scales.* New York: The Psychological Corporation, 1955.

Wright, H. F. Observational child study. In P. Mussen (Ed.), *Handbook of research methods in child development.* New York: Wiley, 1960. Pp. 71-139.

Zigler, E. & Phillips, L. Social effectiveness and symptomatic behaviors. *Journal of Abnormal and Social Psychology,* 1960, 61, 231-238.

8

Conclusion

The cost of "mental illness" is staggering. At all times, between
five and six hundred thousand patients are hospitalized on a
long-term basis in state and federal mental institutions, between
two and three hundred thousand patients are hospitalized for
short periods in private, city and county mental institutions,
and uncounted hundreds of thousands of patients are in treatment with psychotherapists who subscribe to varied theoretical
approaches. The duration of these treatments is measured in
months and years. The cost of these treatments has mounted
steadily, as reflected in a six-fold increase in hospital costs
alone between 1946 and 1966 (Bureau of the Census, 1969,
p. 77). The cost in human suffering and outright economic
loss is inestimable.

In view of the magnitude and expense of these treatments,
one would expect that great care would have gone into their
planning and the evaluation of their effectiveness in order to
insure maximum benefits to patients. The extensive research
reviewed in this book has shown that, compared with patients
who receive no treatment or very limited treatment, those
who receive both in- and out-patient treatment have a small
chance of experiencing marked improvement, a very great
chance of experiencing little or no change and a small chance
of experiencing deterioration. And the indirect negative effects
of psychotherapy may be even greater than the directly
attributable deterioration when the social consequences of
prejudicial labeling are evaluated.

It is possible to ascribe the neutral and negative results of
these treatments to a broad range of factors including, among
others: poor selection or training of therapists; diagnostic and
treatment procedures which are weak in conception or application; and limited therapeutic resources. This book has stressed
only one of these potential sources of difficulty—diagnostic
procedures.

It has been argued that diagnostic systems which seek to
identify inner or dispositional states suffer from low reliability

and validity. The low reliability is a consequence of the fact that extended inferences are made to a large range of unobservable personality characteristics from a small range of observable responses. Because so few elements in the diagnostic process are tied to observable phenomena and so many elements depend upon clinical insight, the outcome of diagnosis is largely under the influence of therapist rather than patient idiosyncrasies. The disjuncture between the client's presenting problem and the diagnosis, the elimination of contextual data from dispositional diagnosis, and the absence of a cogent theory linking diagnosis with treatment procedures and outcome behaviors all contribute to a low level of validity. When treatment is premised upon diagnostic data which is fundamentally unscientific in character (owing to its low reliability and validity), it is unlikely that the treatment can be successful.

It must be admitted that the case against dispositional diagnosis and its applications is as yet incomplete. Some of the studies that reach negative conclusions are weakened by sampling and design problems, and research has yet to be undertaken in certain crucial areas. Despite its weaknesses, the research that reaches negative conclusions in this area tends to be more abundant and more sound than the research that supports the dispositional diagnostic approach.

In view of the vast social and personal costs associated with successful (let alone unsuccessful) treatment, it is reasonable to expect that a profession which consistently experiences negative research results would seek self-corrective action. At least certain members of the "mental health professions" have done so, as represented by the rapid growth in the popularity of behavior therapy, particularly among psychologists. It is nevertheless true that treatments based upon dispositional diagnosis are far more prevalent than those based upon the functional analysis of behavior, and therefore there is a distinct need for immediate change in many treatment programs in this area.

The prospect of a professional response in keeping with the need for change seems dim in light of the remarks made by many proponents of the dispositional diagnostic approach. There are three principal reactions found in the comments of this group. One stresses the reductionist argument that while it is possible to empirically isolate one aspect of a whole for study, this aspect does not give an accurate picture of the whole. The second common reaction is the accusation that critics of the theory do not have access to the entire truth because they lack the same experience as members of the group which is under attack. Both of these arguments are well-illustrated by Saltzman's (1969) response to empirical data which undermine certain psychoanalytic assumptions. He said:

> The best scientific method alone does not make a project scientific. The best scientific method available must grow out of an understanding of the issues involved. Much of the criticism of psychotherapy unfortunately comes from sources that have neither clinical training and orientation nor experience with illness. They are mostly made by academic or clinical psychologists who try to test the validity of a theoretical concept by a statistical study of the outcome of certain procedures [p. 556].

Thus in Saltzman's view, scientific study cannot reveal the true state of affairs and the only people privy to the knowledge needed to make accurate statements are those sharing the author's experiences.

The third set of responses to criticism seeks to suppress (Lehrman, 1960) or ignore (Halleck, 1967) negative findings. Dr. Seymour Halleck (1967), who has been a leading proponent of psychiatric services for adult criminal offenders, observed:

> In spite of the enormous effort that has gone into treatment of the mentally ill, there is no scientific proof of the effectiveness of psychotherapy. . . It must be admitted that there are even less objective data to prove the effectiveness of psychotherapy with offenders than there are with the mentally ill [pp. 338-339].

Nevertheless, seven pages later Dr. Halleck suggested that an ideal correctional program should, among other things:

> . . . expand treatment facilities in correctional institutions . . .
> An increase in the availability of individual psychotherapy,
> group psychotherapy and family psychotherapy is essential to
> an enlightened criminology [pp. 346-347].

Treatment has not worked; therefore expand it!

There are two ways to explain these antiscientific, cultist or illogical responses to negative data. First, psychotherapists are mortal and are subject to the weaknesses of mortals. They may be prisoners of their training to some extent; that is, all have painstakingly acquired a competency through long years of preparation and it takes great character for a man to summarily foresake one skill in order to develop another. In addition, therapists occupy positions of prestige and influence which are richly rewarding. For example, Leifer (1964) has offered the following explanation for the continuation of stress upon psychiatric testimony in criminal hearings:

> The fact that psychiatrists have willingly testified and continue
> to testify in tests of responsibility in spite of these criticisms
> and hazards can be explained by the social advantages, in terms
> of money, prestige, and power, that accrue to psychiatrists and
> to the institution of psychiatry as a result of this activity [p. 827].

Finally, psychotherapists tend to be highly articulate, and a radical shift in position would require public repudiation of formal positions developed over years of teaching, lecturing and writing. This, too, is a difficult obstacle to overcome.

The second explanation for negative responses to contrary data may be that the responses are an expression of frustration. Denied dispositional diagnosis, its proponents may be unaware of the alternative, behavior assessment. Many behavior therapists would identify Skinner's *Science and Human Behavior* (1953) as a major source of stimulation for operant treatment, and Wolpe's *Psychotherapy by Reciprocal Inhibition* (1958) as a major source for respondent treatment. The advent of the explosion in behavior therapy is thus obviously a recent phenomenon, and despite the rapid rise in its popularity it is still a mystery to the vast majority of persons who are working in the field of mental health.

Behavior assessment offers distinct advantages over dispositional diagnosis. It has relatively high reliability and validity and in addition has the advantages of ease, specificity with respect to each patient, objectivity, parsimony, and relevance to treatment. It is hoped that as the techniques of behavior assessment are further developed, through theory development and the use of automated and computer-assisted techniques, the advantages of the approach will become more apparent and it will be more widely used. When this approach is in widespread use, patients will be afforded a measure of protection from unproductive or harmful treatment procedures and professionals will have an ongoing opportunity to increase their effectiveness.

References

Bureau of the Census, U. S. Department of Commerce. *Statistical Abstract of the United States.* Washington, D.C.: U. S. Government Printing Office, 1969.

Halleck, S. L. *Psychiatry and the dilemmas of crime: A study of causes, punishment and treatment.* New York: Harper & Row, 1967.

Lehrman, N. S. Precision in psychoanalysis. *American Journal of Psychiatry,* 1960, 116, 1097-1103.

Leifer, R. The psychiatrist and tests of criminal responsibility. *American Psychologist,* 1964, 19, 825-830.

Saltzman, L. Statistical techniques are premature. *International Journal of Psychiatry,* 1969, 7, 556-558.

Skinner, B. F. *Science and human behavior.* New York: Free Press, 1953.

Wolpe, J. *Psychotherapy by reciprocal inhibition.* Stanford, Calif.: Stanford University Press, 1958.